Seeing

Seeing

How Light Tells Us about the World

Tom Cornsweet

UNIVERSITY OF CALIFORNIA PRESS

University of California Press, one of the most
distinguished university presses in the United States,
enriches lives around the world by advancing scholarship
in the humanities, social sciences, and natural sciences. Its
activities are supported by the UC Press Foundation and
by philanthropic contributions from individuals and
institutions. For more information, visit www.ucpress.edu.

University of California Press
Oakland, California

Library of Congress Cataloging-in-Publication Data

Names: Cornsweet, Tom N., author.
Title: Seeing : how light tells us about the world /
    Tom Cornsweet.
Description: Oakland, California : University of
    California Press, [2017] | Includes bibliographical
    references and index. |
Identifiers: LCCN 2017007238 (print) | LCCN 2017012733
    (ebook) | ISBN 9780520967724 () | ISBN 9780520294646
    (cloth : alk. paper) | ISBN 9780520294639 (pbk. : alk.
    paper)
Subjects: LCSH: Visual perception.
Classification: LCC BF241 (ebook) | LCC BF241 .C654
    2017 (print) | DDC 152.14—dc23
LC record available at https://lccn.loc.gov/2017007238

Manufactured in the United States of America

24 23 22 21 20 19 18 17
10 9 8 7 6 5 4 3 2 1

To Rich Tenney, who asks good questions,
and Ross Beesmer, who is the best at a lot of things,
especially being a friend.

CONTENTS

Preface ix

1. Our Idea of the Physical World

1

2. The Basic Anatomy of the Eye

14

3. How Photoreceptors Sense Light

19

4. Seeing Things That Aren't There

36

5. Not Seeing Things That Are There

43

6. Brightness Constancy

50

7. Why the Rate Of Unbleaching Is Important

59

8. A Little Optics

72

9. Optometrists, Ophthalmologists, Opticians: What They Do

95

10. Color Vision

111

11. Actually Seeing and Not Seeing: Neural Mechanisms

137

Epilogue 165

Appendix: Refraction by Waves 167

Selected Bibliography 181

Index 183

PREFACE

I have been studying, teaching, doing research and engineering in topics related to vision for a very long time, so I decided to write this book to try to answer a few of the questions that people have asked me over the years. Every time I try to do that, to answer a question, I find myself digging deeper and deeper, finding an answer that still has questions in it, answering those and finding that more questions appear. There is never an end to it. I realize, each time, that this is really what doing science is about, trying to understand why—and the why of that—and then of the next that.

Gradually my principal goal in writing this book has changed from trying to answer some questions about vision that I think are interesting to illustrating the process itself of trying to understand. Books on science almost never talk about that. They talk about the results of science— dinosaurs, how the planets move, optical illusions—but they rarely mention the crucial parts, picking things to wonder about that are *worth* wondering about and puzzling over *why* they happen. They are like books on history, which generally only describe history and don't discuss the things that historians actually do to try to figure out what really happened.

So in this book, my main goal is to get you to join me in going deeply into a limited set of aspects of vision that I think are important to understand, and I try to suggest why they are important. Of course we don't ever fully get there. We always end up with more questions.

There are relatively few references to other scientific publications here. Almost all the material that provides background for the discussions has been known for a long time and can be found in many places. What is discussed here is primarily new or, I hope, provides clearer explanations of visual processes that are already well known. For example, if you are reading this book indoors under ordinary reading light and then take it outdoors, the intensity of the light falling on the book and therefore the intensity of the light forming the image of the book on your retinas can easily be a thousand times greater outside, but after a second or two the book looks pretty much the same. At first you probably think, "Why not? It's the same book." But even a rudimentary understanding of what is actually happening reveals that your recognizing this object as something that might be the same thing as the book you were reading indoors reveals some interesting and surprising neural processes.

These processes that have evolved enable our existence and ease our interactions with the physical world as it is on the earth. Most of them result in a good correspondence between our experience and the physical aspects of the world, but when we manipulate those aspects in special ways, we can produce apparent anomalies, like optical illusions. Here, some of these processes will be discussed and analyzed in depth.

CHAPTER ONE

Our Idea of the Physical World

The earth was formed about four billion years ago. During the most recent few hundred thousand years, that is, during the most recent ten-thousandth of the existence of the earth, humans have evolved nervous systems that allow us to sense a little bit, actually a very tiny fraction, of what is going on around us. Our physiological mechanisms of communication—speaking, drawing, writing—have also evolved. As a result of that ability to communicate over time and location, we have been able to accumulate knowledge and understanding of more of the world we live in and to develop means—microscopes, telescopes, radar, X-rays, MRIs—that allow us to sense much more than our physiologies provide.

By far the most immediately useful information about the physical world comes to us directly by means of our senses, especially hearing, vision, and touch. We believe we can sense almost everything that's going on around us, but our senses provide us with an astonishingly small fraction of the information that we are actually imbedded in, and we have generated our conception of the physical world on the basis of the extremely limited range of things in the physical world that can be detected by our physiology.

For instance, we talk as if there are *things,* objects, around us that are fixed and solid—that table, this book—things that are *there.* We say we see this book, but we are actually interacting not with the book but rather with the light reflected from the book. Further, the properties of the book are not at all what our senses tell us. It is made of gigantic quantities of tiny bits, "subatomic particles," that are constantly in motion, with big spaces between them and forces that pull the bits together and push them apart. We talk as though in between objects there is just space, maybe filled with air and sometimes light, but the spaces are actually packed with streams of waves of all kinds of energies, which we know about only because of the accumulation of scientific information gathered from devices that can detect things we can't. Therefore, from our experiences, each of us has put together a concept of the world that is based on a severely restricted portion of the information that is actually present in the physical world, and most of the physiological mechanisms that have evolved in us support that often misleading concept of the world.

Our visual systems have evolved a way of sensing light, which will be discussed at considerable length in the following chapters, and it is a good example of how severely limited our view of the physical world really is. The world is permeated with electromagnetic waves of all kinds. The waves emitted by a typical AM radio transmitter have wavelengths from about 1 meter to about 10,000 meters; X-rays have wavelengths around one ten-thousandth of a millionth (not a typo) of a meter; and various sources, for instance the sun, emit wavelengths at ranges in between. Our eyes have evolved in such a way that we can detect only wavelengths from about 0.4 millionths of a meter to about 0.8 millionths of a meter.

The gap in the middle of figure 1.1 is the way that the range of visible wavelengths is frequently presented. (The row of numbers at the top, labeled "wavelength in meters," is in what is called scientific notation: 10 raised to various exponents. For example, 10^{-12} means 0.000000000001, ten with 11 zeros in front of it.)

The whole width of the drawing represents a range of wavelengths of familiar sources, from gamma rays to radio, and that narrow strip near the middle that is stretched out below represents the range of

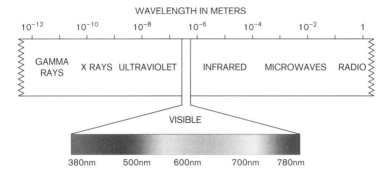

Figure 1.1. Range of wavelengths from gamma rays to radio, with the range of visible wavelengths expanded.

visible wavelengths. That diagram is correct but extremely misleading. Note that the numbers given for wavelength represent what is called a logarithmic scale. That is, each equal space, such as between 10^{-2} (0.01) meters and 1 meter, represents not an equal increase but a 100-fold increase. The distances or lengths in the world we experience are not on a logarithmic scale, and very few people can look at such a scale and understand what it really means.

If, instead, we consider actual lengths or distances, not their logarithms, and we represent the range between AM radio and X-ray wavelengths as the distance from New York to Los Angeles, then the wavelengths we are able to see would be represented on that scale as a distance of less than *an eighth of an inch.* Science had to invent instruments to detect wavelengths represented by the rest of that distance.

Within that extremely restricted visible range of wavelengths, we have evolved physiological devices, called the rod and cone systems, that actually sense different sub-ranges. The rod system is sensitive to one sub-range and the cones to three different sub-ranges, providing us with vision at very low light levels (rods) and in color (cones). Those mechanisms will be discussed in detail in later chapters. We are also limited in the range of brightnesses over which we can see. To understand that limitation, a different aspect of electromagnetic waves will be considered.

A LITTLE BACKGROUND ABOUT LIGHT

To combine, and modify a little, things that Einstein, Bohr, and Feynman have said, "If you think you understand light, you haven't thought deeply enough." Light will be discussed a lot in this book without trying to explain it. But it will be helpful, and not entirely wrong or misleading, to think of light and all other forms of electromagnetic radiation, such as radio waves and X-rays, in the following way.

Water Waves

Try partly filling the bathtub and dropping a pea into the middle of the water. Waves will of course radiate out from where the pea was dropped because the molecules of water under the pea will be pushed down, which will push the molecules next to them away and up, making a rising hump, and since water has the same properties in every direction, it will form in all directions, making a ring. Then those risen molecules will be higher than the rest of the water, so they will push down on their neighbors, making a new ring of humps, and the ring will expand. Meanwhile, the molecules that were pushed down by the pea will be pushed back up by their neighbors, and, having momentum, will keep going up (but not as far as they went down, because of friction among them). Then they will fall back down, starting the cycle over again, each time moving up and down a little less, until the ripples die out.

Why do waves seem to get smaller as they move away from their source? To detect a wave, like the one in the bathtub, the wave has to be detected over some finite part of it. For example, a cork intersects the wave over the width of the cork and detects the wave by its up-and-down motion. Similarly, if you look at a wave to try to determine its height, you only make the height judgment by watching a short stretch of the wave. Each wave forms a circle that expands as it travels away from its source, so the farther a wave has traveled, the greater is its radius and the smaller is the proportion of the wave that will be detected.

Because the circumference of a circle increases in direct proportion to its radius (circumference = pi × radius × 2), the proportion of the energy in a water wave that is detected is inversely proportional to the distance it has traveled. (That's not quite true with a water wave in a bathtub because the molecules of water exert a little friction on each other, which uses up some of the energy that the pea transferred to the water. A wave in the ocean can gather energy from wind and differences in water temperature, and so usually doesn't get smaller as it travels.)

That is a very crude and not quite accurate description of why water waves radiate out from a dropped pea, making a little group of rings that decrease in height as they travel away from the center, but it's a start on an explanation of electromagnetic waves.

Now suppose you want to detect or sense the water wave. You might put a cork in the water and measure how it moves up and down as the wave passes. The distance the cork travels up and then down is a measure of the strength, really the *amplitude,* of the wave at that particular place, and the number of times the cork moves up and down each second is the *frequency* of the wave at that point. If you have two corks and move one farther away from the center of the wave than the other until the two corks are moving up and down together, as in figure 1.2, the distance between the corks is what's called the *wavelength* of the wave.

Here are some more words and concepts that are useful in understanding waves. A *force* is a push or pull against an object. *Energy* is basically defined as the amount of whatever it is that moves something against a force. For the water wave, since the water molecules are pushed and pulled by the force of gravity, the wave must carry energy, but figuring out how much is a little tricky. You can weigh the cork and measure its amplitude of movement, which gives you a measure of energy, but that is just sampling the energy in the short segment of the wave that intersects the cork. That is just the energy that hits the cork. To have a measure of the energy of the entire wave, all the vertical movements should be added around the entire circumference of the wave.

Figure 1.2. Water waves with corks marking crests. The distance between corks is the wavelength.

Light and Other Electromagnetic Waves

Suppose somebody hands you two objects, one to hold in each hand, and you find that you have to make an effort to hold them apart; they keep trying to get together. Or you have to exert effort to keep them from flying apart. The experience of that effort is what physicists call *force*. You have to exert a force to keep them from coming together or moving apart.

It is critically important to be clear about the subtle distinction between how we conceive of the world and what we actually observe. For example, the first few sentences in the preceding paragraph could have said "A force is strength or energy as an attribute of physical action or movements," or "A force is a push or pull upon an object resulting from the object's interaction with another object," both quotes from definitions of "force" on the internet. But that kind of sentence implies that there are forces, things, out there. No one has seen piles of forces lying around. Instead, scientists have observed the behaviors of objects, have had experiences, and have given the experiences names. Making this important distinction often requires somewhat awkward and wordy sentences, but it is worth it. In fiction brevity is elegant. In explanations, it can sometimes be confusing.

If you have exerted force over some distance, you have expended *energy*. The definition of energy is the exertion of a force over a distance. An object is said to have *potential* energy if there is a force acting on it but it doesn't move, and *kinetic* energy if there is a force acting on it and it does move. When electromagnetic energy, for example light, travels through a vacuum—think of it as fast-traveling packets of energy—nothing pushes against it and it doesn't push against anything, but if it hits an object, it will transfer some or all of its energy to the object, making the object move (or move in a different way than it was already moving), and that requires energy. So we say that a beam of light traveling in a vacuum has potential energy, and if it hits something, some or all of that energy becomes kinetic energy.

We describe matter as made up of things we call atoms. Some of the things all atoms contain are called electrons, and others are called protons; atoms of different materials normally contain different numbers of electrons and protons. Protons exert forces against each other but attract electrons, and electrons exert forces against each other but attract protons.

Usually, the forces among electrons and protons in the atoms that make up any object are balanced. However, it's easy to spoil that balance. For instance, walk across a carpet on a dry day, shuffling your feet a little. That will rub off some of the electrons from the atoms in the carpet and attach them to your feet, giving you more electrons than are balanced by your protons, and those extra electrons, pushing against each other, will spread over your whole body. Then if you touch a doorknob or your dog, unless they happen to have the same imbalance between electrons and protons, your electrons will push the extra electrons to the knob or dog in the form of a spark of "static electricity."

When an object has more electrons than it would at balance, it is said to have a negative charge. Too few electrons create a positive charge. All these words have been leading up to describing what creates an electromagnetic wave. *Whenever an object has a charge and it moves, a particular kind of wave, an electromagnetic wave, is emitted* and travels off. If you walk across a carpet, picking up electrons, and then wave your hand back and forth, you generate an electromagnetic wave. The *frequency* of the wave equals the number of times you wave back and forth per second, and the *amplitude* of the wave is proportional to the distance your hand travels in each cycle.

The electromagnetic waves your charged hand makes travel away at the speed of light (very slightly slower in air than in a vacuum), so each movement back and then forth creates a wave that goes back and then forth over some distance, the *wavelength*. For instance, if your hand made one complete cycle back and forth in a hundredth of a second (so the frequency of the electromagnetic wave is a hundred cycles per second) and it travels 300,000,000 meters per second, its wavelength is 300,000,000/100 = 3,000,000 meters.

(We don't actually observe the wave traveling from the source to its detector. We observe that when a charge moves, some time later a detector responds, and there is a delay between the movement and the detection that depends on the distance between the two. Whatever it is that traveled from the source to the detector exhibits some properties of waves that we can observe, for instance water waves—and some properties of particles, as will be discussed below.)

Radio broadcasting stations have electronic devices that cause electrons to move back and forth and emit wavelengths in the neighborhood of one meter. Cell phones transmit and receive signals at about three-tenths of a meter. Wi-Fi is about one-tenth of a meter. Visible electromagnetic radiation, which we call light, has wavelengths between about 0.4 millionths of a meter and 0.8 millionths of a meter. X-rays have wavelengths in the neighborhood of one ten-thousandth of a millionth of a meter. All electromagnetic waves have the same basic properties; they are waves of energy of different frequencies and amplitudes, traveling extremely fast. Our space is crammed full of electromagnetic waves traveling in all directions, but, as shown in figure 1.1, our physiology is capable of sensing only a very narrow range of them.

In many ways, electromagnetic energy acts as water waves do. However, when electromagnetic waves are being detected, they act as though they consist of a stream of separate packets of energy, like bullets. Suppose the amplitude of the light wave, where it hits the detector, is extremely small. The kinds of devices used to detect light contain a material that converts the energy in light into what we can think of as shifts in the position of one or more electrons in the molecules of the material, and the physics of that material permits electrons to shift only among a limited number of positions. (These "positions" are usually called energy levels.) As a result, an extremely weak wave may not deliver enough energy to shift even one electron, and the presence of the wave may not be detected.

If, as it intersects the detector, the wave has a little more energy, it may trigger the shift of one or maybe two electrons, and as the energy contained in the portion of the wave intersecting the detector increases, the *number* of electron shifts or jumps will increase. If the energy in a wave is too small to shift an electron in a detector, there is no way to know whether or not the wave is actually present, so we say there was no wave, or if it has enough energy to shift some number of electrons but not enough to shift that number plus one, then we say that the amount of light, when it's being detected, increases in steps. It acts as though it consists of particles of energy.

The physics of this process does not allow the shifting of a fraction of an electron. Therefore, the intensity of a light wave must be described or measured as a whole number of shifts per unit of time. (The reason some subatomic particles have charges—and as a result the shifts in electrons are constrained to a limited number of positions or levels—is one of those deep spots into which we will try to avoid stepping.) So when light is detected, it is as if the light is a stream of particles of energy, unlike the way a wave behaves. These particles of energy are called *quanta,* and the kinds of quanta that we can see, quanta of light, are usually called *photons.*

A light wave traveling though empty space expands as a sphere. For it to be detected, its energy must be absorbed over an area, that is, over a two-dimensional detector such as a solar cell, a pixel in a camera, or a photodetector in the eye. The area of the surface of a sphere increases in proportion to the square of its radius. Therefore, so long as the area of the detector doesn't change, the energy it detects will be inversely proportional to the square of the distance between it and the source. Imagine how much energy is being emitted by the nearest visible star (other than our sun), which is the third-brightest star in the night sky and about 25,000,000,000,000 miles away. For us to see it, it must emit enough energy *in all directions* so that when it passes through a hole six or so millimeters in diameter (your pupil), it stimulates your retina strongly enough that you can see it.

Not only is human vision limited to a small range of wavelengths, it is also limited to a range of *intensities.* If you've been in darkness for about a half hour or more, a small source of light has to deliver about five or ten photons to your eye in about a tenth of a second for you to reliably detect it. At the lower end of the range of intensities of human vision, if you've been in darkness for a while, you could detect the approach of an albino lion on a moonless night with a cloudy sky.

At the other end of the range, after you've been looking for a few seconds, you can see well on a beach or snow field at noon, when the illumination is at least a billion times as intense. So human vision operates over a range of intensities of at least 1,000,000,000-fold.

But in order for us to do what we call seeing, we need information not just about whether or not light is falling on our retinas, but also about the distribution of the light in the scene. (Image formation and the ways that our eyes perform it will be discussed in chapter 8.)

For example, suppose you are outside on a clear night lit by a full moon, and the range of intensities falling on your retina in the image of the scene is from 1,000 photons per second in the dimmest place to

100,000 per second in the brightest place. Then suddenly the street lights are turned on. That will increase the illumination on the scene about 100-fold. During the first second or two after the street lights are turned on, everything will look equally bright. No detail will be visible. But then, photochemical processes (discussed in later chapters) will quickly shift the 100-fold range of vision upward, so that the range becomes from 100,000 to 10,000,000 photons per second, and you will be able to see detail again. That shift is called *light adaptation.* A change in illumination in the opposite direction—the street lights suddenly going off—produces the opposite effect, *dark adaptation,* but the downward shift in range is significantly slower.

Despite the processes of light and dark adaptation, the range of levels of illumination over which we humans can see is still somewhat limited—owls can see well at significantly lower light levels than we can.

The upper limit of the range of intensities over which our visual systems operate depends on the wavelength of the light. Two quite different mechanisms determine this limit. As explained in detail in chapter 3, when visual pigment molecules absorb light, they change their form to one that no longer absorbs light. They are said to be *bleached.* Therefore, for some wavelengths, the upper limit is reached when the light is so intense that essentially all the visual pigment molecules are in that bleached state. However, for most wavelengths—those outside or near the edges of the small range of vision indicated in figure 1.1—high intensities will cause the tissues of the retina to boil before they become great enough to bleach essentially all the pigment, setting an upper limit in a more permanent way.

Very few situations occur on Earth under which the natural levels of illumination exceed our normal range. Looking at the sun is one of them.

STARING AT THE SUN CAN CAUSE PERMANENT EYE DAMAGE.

Limitations in the range of operation exist in all of our sense modalities. For example, until undersea sound sensors were developed, we were unaware of the very long-wavelength (low-frequency) sounds emitted and sensed by whales and the very short-wavelength (high-frequency) clicks generated by crustaceans that abound in the depths of the ocean. Mechanisms to sense those frequencies had little survival value in the evolution of humans.

We call carbon monoxide odorless, but that is not a property of the gas, it is a limitation of our olfactory systems. If carbon monoxide occurred with much abundance on the earth, we would probably have evolved a biological detector. Glossy paper feels smooth, but under a microscope the roughness of its texture becomes obvious.

As discussed above, the range of all the wavelengths in the universe that we can actually use to see is extremely limited, and we will examine the reasons for this limitation at the molecular level in later chapters.

THINGS TO THINK ABOUT

There will be a few questions following each chapter. You might find answers to some of these questions in later chapters, but don't go looking for those answers now. Try to answer the questions yourself. You will probably be tempted to look for answers on the internet. Be warned that most of the "information" in cyberspace is simply wrong.

Often, we think we understand an issue until we try to explain it. How many times have teachers heard, "I know the answer but I just can't put it into words." Baloney! You don't know the answer until you *can* put it into words. Write down your answers to these questions or try to explain them to someone else.

1. Bees can see light of wavelengths shorter than we can see, that is, *ultraviolet.* Further, pictures of some flowers, when taken with a camera that is sensitive to ultraviolet light, show strong bull's-eye-like patterns that are not visible to the human eye. Do you think that bees' eyes and those flowers evolved together or that one came before the other, and if so, which came first? Can you be explicit about the reasoning behind your belief?

2. Here's another way to get a feeling for logarithmic scales. Suppose you could save a thousand dollars (10^3) every year in a box under your bed. How many years would it take you to save up a million dollars (10^6)? (In hundred-dollar bills, this would be a stack 43 inches high.) If you could save a million dollars a year, how many years would it take you to save up a billion dollars (10^9)? How high would that stack be? (The tallest building in the world, in 2017, is 32,664 inches high.)

RELEVANT READING

Even though it is more than fifty years old, for a clear explanation of the physical principles underlying optics (and for all of physics), there is nothing better than the Feynman Lectures:

Richard Phillips Feynman, Robert B. Leighton, and Matthew Sands. 1963. *The Feynman Lectures on Physics.* Addison-Wesley.

CHAPTER TWO

The Basic Anatomy of the Eye

You are probably familiar with the general structure of the human eye-ball. As a refresher, and to remind you of the meaning of some of the terms that will be used in the chapters that follow, a cross-section is shown in figure 2.1 and will be briefly reviewed here.

Light first encounters the cornea, a transparent curved tissue about half a millimeter (about one-fiftieth of an inch) thick. Light then passes through a fluid that is only slightly different from water, called the aqueous humor, and arrives at the plane of the iris, a colored group of muscles. The muscles surround a hole, the pupil. If photons hit the iris, they are absorbed by pigment molecules there and have no effect on vision. (In some animals, for example the frog, light falling on the iris does produce a response, but not in humans.) Photons passing through the pupil encounter a lens, sometimes called the crystalline lens, then a transparent jelly-like medium called the vitreous gel or vitreous humor, and finally they fall on a layer of neural tissue, the retina. Lenses can form images, of course, and images are formed on the retina, as explained in chapter 8. The cornea provides about two-thirds of the optical power to form retinal images, and the crystalline lens adds the other third. (The macula and fovea are specialized regions of the retina that will be discussed later.)

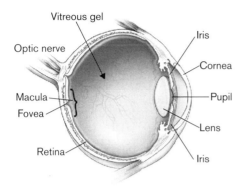

Figure 2.1. The human eye.

The retina is about half a millimeter thick and is made up of several layers. One of those layers consists of specialized cells, the *photoreceptors,* which contain visual pigment. The bottom layer, that is, the layer farthest from the front of the eye, contains blood vessels and dark nonvisual pigment, and the layers between the photoreceptor layer and the front of the eye consist of transparent neural tissue that acts like part of the brain, processing the outputs of the photoreceptors and sending signals through the optic nerve to the brain. (Some of the functions performed by these layers will be discussed in chapter 11.) So photons pass through the cornea, the pupil, the lens, the vitreous humor, and the top neural layers of the retina, and arrive at the photoreceptor layer, where they are detected, and then the resulting signals are conducted by optic nerves to the brain.

As discussed at length in chapter 3, each molecule of pigment in the photoreceptors is, like all molecules, a structure made up of atoms, and each atom is a structure of subatomic particles. All those particles are held together in particular arrangements by forces called bonds. When a photon arrives at a pigment molecule, it may or may not "fit" the molecule, that is, it may or may not be absorbed by the molecule, depending upon whether the photon has just the right amount of energy to "fit" into the structure of the molecule. If it does not fit, the photon passes through, but if it does fit, it is likely to cause the molecule to change its shape, which triggers a cascade of electrochemical events, producing a signal that is sent to the brain. (About 70 percent of the molecules that absorb a photon change their shape. The remaining 30 percent just temporarily heat up a little and do not contribute to vision.)

During fetal development, a patch on the surface of the human embryo will become the brain, and two small pieces of that patch grow out on stalks and form the retinas. So the retinas are, in a way, part of the brain, and they do an important portion of the image processing that causes us to see what we see, as we will examine in chapter 11.

Almost all of the area in the back of the eye is covered with photoreceptors, and each receptor contains a million or more molecules of visual pigment, so if a photon arrives at the retina and has the right amount of energy, it is likely to be absorbed and trigger a neural process that leads to our seeing.

THE PUPIL AND ITS ROLE IN VISION

Why do people have pupils? Of course there has to be a transparent hole of some kind to let light through to the retina, but why do pupils change size, and why do some animals have pupils with different shapes, like the slit pupils of a cat?

The visual system drives the iris muscles to make the pupils smaller when the scene is brighter. If when going from a dark scene to a brighter one the diameter of the pupil shrinks by, say, half, the area through which light from the scene gets to the retina will be reduced to one-fourth, and therefore the amount of light heading to the retina from each point in the scene will be reduced by a factor of four. So it seems as if changes in pupil size compensate for changes in scene brightness, keeping the light intensity at the retina constant. But the brightness in a normally lighted room can be one-thousandth of the normal brightness outside during the day, while the biggest that a human pupil can get is about 8 millimeters in diameter (about 0.3 inches) and the smallest about 2 millimeters (about 0.08 inches), a change in diameter of four to one and therefore a change in area of sixteen to one. That is, even under ordinary conditions, the human pupil can correct for at most a sixtieth of the change in brightness between outdoors and inside. And if you are in a room lighted just enough that you can see things and then you go out to the beach on a sunny day, the change in scene brightness can be a billion to one or more, so the human pupil doesn't even come close to being able to correct for ordinary changes in the brightness of a scene. (Cats have slit pupils, which allows the areas of their pupils to change from all the way open to all the way closed, so their pupils can compensate for any amount of change in scene brightness.)

When the eye is suddenly exposed to a bright light, the pupil will compensate a little, but the photoreceptors in the retina will still be exposed to a huge change in the intensity of the light falling on them, a change bigger than the physiological mechanisms that send signals to the brain can handle, so the scene at first will seem blindingly bright. After a few seconds, it will still appear bright, but not blindingly, that is, you can see different things in the scene. (The pupils can go from as large as they can get to as small as they can get in a fraction of a second, and changes in the photoreceptors themselves, which are responsible for almost all of the change in brightness, take only a few seconds to occur. Those changes in the photoreceptors will be discussed extensively in chapters 3 and 7.)

When you go into a darkened movie theater, at first it seems too dark to see anything, but after a few minutes things are easy to see. What's happening is that the photoreceptors and the organization of the neurons connected to the receptors change their sensitivity, so in a bright scene the retina is much less sensitive than after you've been in the dark for a while. That process, the change in sensitivity of the eye under different lighting conditions, is called *adaptation*.

So what good are pupils? The main function of human pupils seems to be that they furnish a subject of study for people doing vision research. But changes in pupil size do provide one important function. Large pupils let more light enter the eyes, so they help a little in seeing under dim lighting, but when the pupil is large, the light forming the retinal image passes through a larger segment of the optical surfaces of the eye, so more defects in the shapes of those surfaces affect the image and reduce its sharpness, reducing acuity. In bright light, the pupils constrict and therefore can significantly improve acuity. In addition, if something is out of focus, for instance if you are near-sighted and looking at a distant scene without wearing your glasses, the amount of blurring caused by the poor focus will be reduced when the pupil is smaller, for reasons that will be explained in chapter 8. (As a consequence of the statistics of the arrival of photons at the retina and changes in the neural organization of retinal processing, even if the pupil did not change size, increasing the light level improves acuity, so long as the upper limit of the retinal response is not exceeded.)

As we will examine in chapter 8, the cornea and lens in the eye act on the light from the scene to produce an image of the scene on the retina. You can think of the scene as a distribution of light intensities and wavelengths, and the image on the retina is essentially a tiny copy of that distribution. Different intensities and wavelengths fall on different photoreceptors in the retina, and those receptors send signals to the brain that correspond to the nature of the light falling on them. In the following chapters, the processes that produce those signals will be analyzed.

THINGS TO THINK ABOUT

Eye doctors look into your eye to see the retina. They usually use a device called an ophthalmoscope. How does it work? (The light reflected from the front surface of the cornea is much brighter than the light from the retina and masks the view of the retina, so the ophthalmoscope has to be built to prevent that masking.)

CHAPTER THREE

How Photoreceptors Sense Light

When we say we have the feeling that we "understand" some phenomenon, we usually mean that we think about it in terms of things or events that we have actually experienced. For instance, we "understand" that gasses are made up of molecules that are constantly moving, and that when those molecules bump against the walls of a container, the bumping pushes on the walls. We label that "pressure." Although we don't actually see the molecules, we imagine balls bumping into walls, which we have seen, and the explanation gives us the feeling that we understand, at least roughly, what we mean by pressure, molecules, and so on.

All of the visual phenomena discussed in this book depend, initially, on the events and processes that occur when light interacts with the light detectors in our eyes, so this chapter is an attempt to provide an understanding of those events.

The entire surface of the retina (except for a small part called the optic disk) is covered with photoreceptors: tiny tubes filled with visual pigment molecules, each pigment molecule being embedded in a membrane. First, assume that nothing is moving except the incoming photons. That assumption *cannot be correct* but it is useful as a first step in developing an understanding of what goes on.

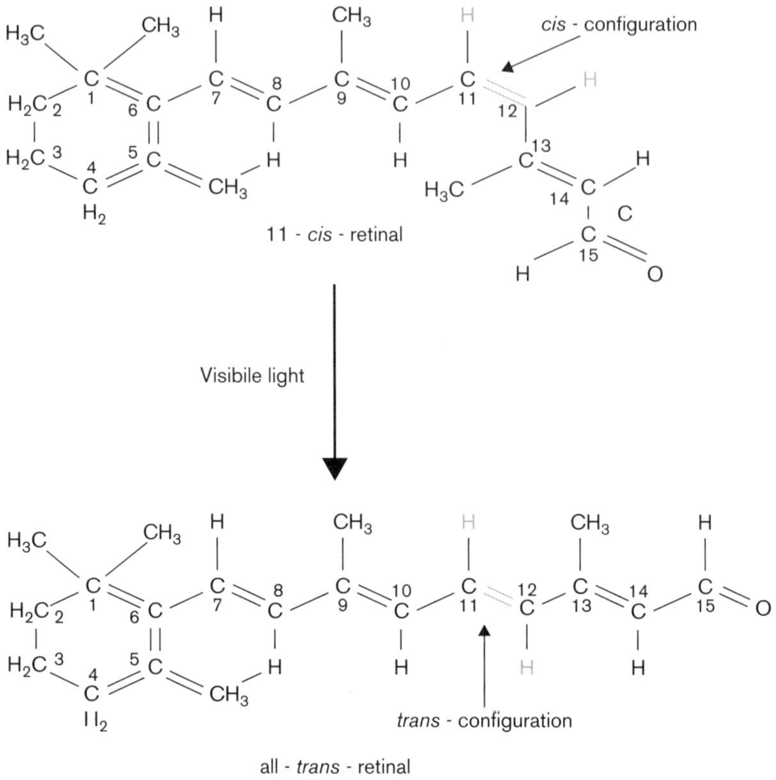

Figure 3.1. The two states of the chemical structure of a visual pigment molecule.

Suppose a photon of just the right wavelength and energy strikes a molecule in just the right place and at just the right angle, so that the photon exactly "fits" the molecule, and the energy in the photon is transferred to the molecule. When that happens, the energy in the photon causes one of the bonds between atoms in the molecule to change, and as a consequence, the molecule changes its shape a little. Before absorbing a photon, the molecule can be thought of as bent at that bond, and if the molecule absorbs a photon, the energy in the photon changes the bond and the molecule isomerizes, it straightens. The two states, isomers, of visual pigment molecules are diagrammed in figure 3.1.

This straightening has two important results. First, when the molecule straightens, it reduces the size of hole in the membrane that it's imbedded in. Second, the change in shape, which is also a change in the distribution of charges and bonds within the molecule, changes the "fit." That is, the energy in each of the photons that fit the bent molecule no longer fits the straightened one. The straightened one is transparent to the kind of photons that it originally absorbed—the molecule is "bleached." (Photons of significantly greater energy and shorter wavelength would now fit the straightened molecule, while the photons of the original kind sail right through. But these shorter-wavelength photons are absorbed by the cornea and crystalline lens before they can even get to the visual pigment molecules.)

Wavelength and energy are reciprocally related in a photon. Imagine two photons, one with a short wavelength and the other with one twice as long. Assuming that the speed of travel of both photons is about the same, it will take about the same, very short, time for each photon to pass through a pigment molecule, and while passing through, the photon with the shorter wavelength (and therefore the greater frequency) will go through twice as many cycles as the one with the longer wavelength, thus exposing the molecule to twice as much energy. The wavelength of a photon can sort of be thought of as its size, and the distribution of atoms in the pigment molecule thought of as a shape or size that fits, or doesn't.

Figure 3.2 is a plot of what might be expected when a photon hits a pigment molecule in just the right way, and has exactly the right energy or wavelength to fit, under the erroneous assumption that nothing is moving except the photon. The horizontal axis represents the wavelength of the photon. That is, moving rightward along the horizontal axis, the plot shows what would happen to photons of increasing wavelength (and decreasing energy). The vertical axis represents the likelihood or probability that a photon at each of the wavelengths on the horizontal axis would be absorbed by the pigment molecule and cause it to change its shape, to isomerize. In this special unrealistic case, the molecule would absorb photons of only a single wavelength.

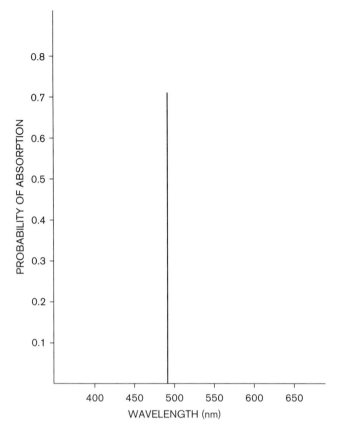

Figure 3.2. What the absorption spectrum of a visual pigment molecule would look like if all atomic motion were eliminated. Such motion cannot be eliminated.

However, all the tiny elements of matter are always in motion. Therefore, the structure of the pigment molecule and the relationships among the forces holding it together will always be fluctuating a little, and different photons will hit the molecule at slightly different places and from different directions. As result, the curve relating the probability of absorption to the wavelength of the photon will broaden. Figure 3.3 is a plot of the actual probability of absorption of one of the pigments in our photoreceptors. This kind of plot is called an *absorption spectrum,* and the

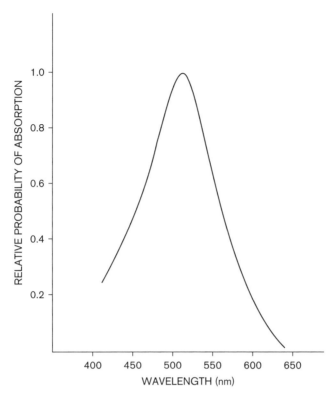

Figure 3.3. The actual absorption spectrum of the visual pigment in human rods.

one in figure 3.3 is the absorption spectrum of the visual pigment in a class of receptors called rods. (The other kind, cones, will be extensively discussed in later chapters.)

In this kind of plot, the units of the numbers on the horizontal axis, wavelength, are given in nanometers (nm), a nanometer being a thousandth of a millionth of a meter. The vertical axis is not as straightforward. The ideal scale for the vertical axis would be the probability that a photon at a wavelength along the horizontal axis would be absorbed by a single molecule of pigment, but that would be extremely difficult to measure. Instead, the measurement is made by passing a large number of photons of each wavelength through a chamber filled with an unknown number of millions of pigment molecules, and plotting the results so that the wavelength with the greatest proportion of photons absorbed is arbitrarily called 1.00 on the vertical axis; thus the label on the vertical axis is "*relative* probability of absorption."

As described above, when a visual pigment molecule absorbs a photon, it isomerizes, and that triggers a cascade of neural events that results in signals being sent to the brain. The isomerization also causes the absorption spectrum of the molecule to shift strongly in such a way that it becomes transparent to the wavelengths in figure 3.3: it bleaches. So figure 3.3 is a plot of the absorption spectrum of rod pigment when the pigment is in its bent state. As mentioned earlier, the entire curve shifts toward absorption at shorter wavelengths if a molecule absorbs a photon and straightens, and the wavelengths it shifts to are ones that are absorbed by parts of the eye, such as the cornea and lens, before they can get to the retina. (The absorption spectrum of window glass is such that the wavelengths that affect our retinas are absorbed to a negligible degree but quanta of shorter wavelengths, ultraviolet, are absorbed strongly. Bricks and sheetrock absorb visible wavelengths but transmit long wavelengths, such as radio and cellphone waves.)

All the tiny constituents of all molecules and atoms are constantly in motion. When a visual pigment molecule is in its bent state and is surrounded by the nutrients that arrive in blood, even in darkness there is always a chance that the energy in the motion of the surroundings will cause an isomerization to its straightened state. That is, a visual signal can be triggered by a non-visual event. That probability is very low, and the bent state is said to be stable, but there are a million or more pigment molecules in each receptor, so the probability that a bent molecule in a receptor will straighten in the absence of a photon is not zero, and therefore the chances of seeing tiny flashes when you are in a totally dark room is not zero. How you can see those flashes and what they look like will be discussed in chapter 4. (Imagine a very high-energy quantum, an X-ray or gamma ray quantum coming from outer space, that hits and fits a molecule in a double helix in one of your genes, changing your genetic coding. Maybe you don't want to imagine that, but it is probably a necessary step in evolution.)

The visual pigment molecules in rods and cones are imbedded in slightly different environments, but for both, in the presence of the nutrients in those environments, the straightened state is much less stable than the bent state. If you were to watch a straightened, that is bleached, rod pigment molecule in complete darkness, it might "spontaneously" jump back to its bent state at any time. The actual time is unpredictable, but on average, you would have to watch it for about seven minutes before it bent. If you watched a million straight rod pigment molecules in darkness, you would see that half of them would have bent in about seven minutes, half of what was left in another seven minutes, and so on, until after about forty minutes in complete darkness, almost all of the rod pigment molecules would be in their bent state. (Not all of them would be bent, because bent ones "spontaneously" straighten. They just do so at a much lower rate.) The corresponding time for about half of the bleached *cone* pigment molecules to "unbleach" is less than one minute. (These times have been studied only for limited regions of the retina; it is possible that the times are different in regions that have not been studied, such as regions far from the center of the retina.)

It is a basic element of modern physics, that is, quantum mechanics, that all of the tiny components of matter are constantly in motion. There may not be a satisfying explanation about why that is true (another deep spot that we will avoid stepping into), but it is fundamental. The consequences of that motion are often called "spontaneous," as in the preceding paragraph, but the word "spontaneous" implies that the reason an event occurred is not or cannot be known, while most such events, including the occasional bleaching of an unbleached pigment molecule in darkness and the more frequent unbleaching of a bleached molecule, are almost certainly a result of the exchange of energy between the molecule and its surrounding, moving, particles of matter, so the term "spontaneous" will be replaced by "QM" in the remainder of this book, signifying a consequence of a quantum-mechanical event.

Obviously, that QM return of straightened molecules to their bent, sensitive state causes a corresponding increase in overall sensitivity to light, and the change in sensitivity is called *dark adaptation* (and the corresponding decrease in sensitivity when the lighting increases is called *light adaptation*). In the classic example, when you first enter a darkened movie theater you can see very little, but after a few minutes things become visible again. That is a good example of dark adaptation.

It is not at all obvious why the bleaching and QM unbleaching of visual pigment molecules should increase the range of useful light intensities. However, the return of straight molecules to their bent state is critical in determining the range of light intensities over which the human visual system can operate effectively, as will be analyzed in chapter 7. The range is actually about a *billion* to one. (That range holds so long as the eyes have time to light- or dark-adapt. The range for discriminating among different intensities in a single flash is closer to a hundred to one.) Several factors contribute to the breadth of that range, and they will be discussed later, but a major contributor is related to the bleaching and unbleaching of pigment molecules.

In man-made light-sensing devices, such as solar cells or cameras, the first step in photon detection is fundamentally the same as described above for visual pigments. That is, if an arriving photon "fits" the structure of a molecule in the detector, the photon is absorbed and produces a signal. (In a camera, the equivalent of the visual "absorption spectrum" is usually called the "spectral sensitivity curve".) However, in a camera the absorbing molecule does not bleach and is instantly ready to absorb another photon. That lack of bleaching makes a huge difference in the behavior of the sensor, so that, for instance, the range of intensities over which the image in a camera can be sensed is typically about 250 to 1, and sometimes as high as 1,000 to 1. (Remember that the range for human vision is about 1,000,000 to 1.) Don't take the numbers in this comparison too seriously. A proper comparison would take into account the tricks that camera manufacturers and photographers might do, the fact that people can put on sunglasses, and so on; a full discussion would be far more complicated than is appropriate here.

HOW SENSITIVE IS A DARK-ADAPTED HUMAN RETINA? HOW DO YOU FIND OUT?

Of course you will need some apparatus—at least a light source, a means of adjusting its intensity, a means of measuring the intensity, and more, as you will see. You will probably want to project the light onto some surface and be able to measure the intensity reflected from it.

Begin by putting a subject into a completely dark room or covering their eyes with a completely opaque blindfold for at least forty minutes, so that almost all of their visual pigment molecules are in their bent, sensitive state. (There will always be some that have been changed back to their straightened, insensitive, state by the QM energy in their surroundings.)

Then you might simply turn the intensity down to zero, ask the subject to look at the surface, gradually turn the intensity up, and ask the subject to tell you as soon as they see it. Although at first that seems like the obvious procedure, there are a lot of things wrong with it. One problem is that the subject can't tell you it is visible until after it becomes visible, and since the intensity is gradually rising, the actual intensity when it was first seen will depend on how fast you are raising it and the subject's reaction time.

So you need to be able to deliver the light in flashes. You need to add to your apparatus a means of delivering flashes, let's say flashes one second long and delivered with enough delay between them that the subject has time to consider and then respond before the next flash. Then you could set each successive flash to a higher intensity until the subject reports seeing it.

How should the intensity be varied? You might gradually turn a knob that adjusts the intensity, but there is a serious problem with that method. If the experimenter is adjusting the intensity, his or her expectations can strongly influence the result. A famous physiologist, who will not be named here, provided a typical example. He published more than a hundred papers in reputable scientific journals describing studies that supported various aspects of his theory, but other scientists were unable to replicate his results. He did not bother to describe, in his papers, the method of data collection he used. When he was finally asked to describe his method, he reported it as follows. He turned a knob that smoothly adjusted a parameter of interest, for example, the intensity of a test spot, and asked the subject to report when some property, for example the color of the spot, was first seen. But he turned the knob rapidly over regions that he "knew" did not include the threshold value, and slowed down in regions where he expected the threshold to be, so that his measures would be more precise—a natural thing to do. Further studies, by other scientists, showed clearly that subjects were far more likely to respond when the rate of change was slowed. (One reason is simply that, if the intensity is changed slowly, the subject spends more time looking at stimuli and trying to decide whether or not to respond, and so is more likely to respond. The result is an increase is "seen" responses at the expected intensities.) Therefore, all of that scientist's results erroneously fit his theories. He subsequently ceased working on issues related to vision.

A better way to do it would be to add another component to the apparatus that delivers flashes of, say, eight different intensities in steps between zero and easily seen, in a random order, and to record whether or not the subject reported seeing each flash. A computer could perform this procedure. (You would need to add a means by which the subject could report the judgement to the computer.) The result of that procedure might look like figure 3.4. But if it does, it means that the steps in intensity were too big. The "threshold" might be any intensity between 30 and 40 (for this example, assume, just for convenience, that the unit of intensity along the horizontal axis are numbers of photons arriving at the pupil per square millimeter per second), so the method isn't very sensitive, but at least you got a ball-park estimate of the threshold.

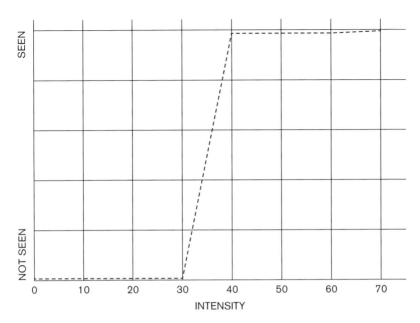

Figure 3.4. An example of the results of an experiment to determine the sensitivity to a flash of light, when the change in intensity between stimuli is large.

So, redo the measurement but using intensities between, say, 25 and 40. Then the results will probably look like those in figure 3.5. Repeat the procedure and the result will be similar but not exactly the same. There is variability!

Why is there variability in the results, that is, why don't the results come out exactly the same every time? If there were no variability, you would only need to test each intensity once. But there is always variability in any proper measurement. (The mass of an electron has been determined to nine decimal places, but there is still uncertainty about the tenth.) There are two main sources of variability in the measurement of the threshold for seeing a flash when the subject is dark-adapted. One is variability in the subject's sensitivity, and the other is variability in the stimulus itself.

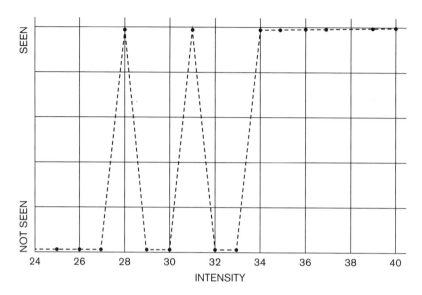

Figure 3.5. The results when the change in intensity between flashes is small.

The variability in the subject is generated by QM variations in the activity of neurons in the retina and brain, as well as factors more difficult to identify, like variations in attention, or in expectations about what might happen next. The variability in the stimulus is also related to quantum mechanics. The number of photons that even a perfect light source emits in any fixed period of time will vary. Photons are emitted by a process that is inherently random. When the light being measured is intense, that is, when the rate of detection is high, this variability is a small fraction of the average rate, so the variability of any measure of its intensity is a small percentage of the measure, but at low intensities the variability becomes significant. Specifically, the number of photons emitted by a "steady" source and detected in a particular time interval will vary with a spread that is directly proportional to the square root of the average (called a Poisson distribution). Since the number of photons required to see a test flash when the eye is dark-adapted is very small, the square root of that small number will be a

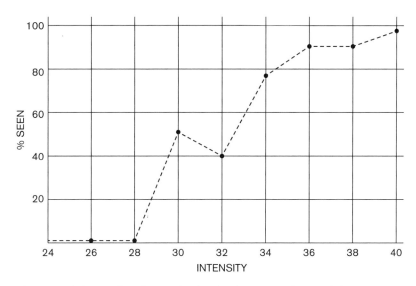

Figure 3.6. The results when each stimulus is presented several times.

substantial proportion of the number itself, so the actual number of photons delivered to the eye will vary significantly from flash to flash.

To lessen the uncertainty about what the threshold really is, repeat the procedure again, but this time, include ten flashes at each of the intensities. The result might look like the one in figure 3.6. Note that the vertical axis is now labeled "% seen." In general, the more times you repeat the procedure, the smoother and more consistent the resulting curve will be.

What do you do with that result? How do you relate it to the question of the sensitivity of human vision? You might choose the intensity for which the subject says the flash is seen 50 percent of the time, or 75 percent. But that is not quite the answer to the original question. It is an answer to the question, "At what intensity setting will the subject say the flash is seen?" But you will get one answer if you instruct the subject to be really sure and a different answer if you ask when it can just barely be seen. The subject has to make a judgement, and so the result will depend on the subject's idea of what "seeing" means. That might be

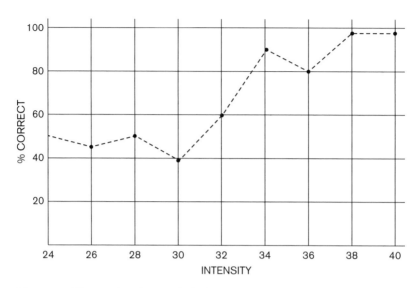

Figure 3.7. The results when each flash is presented many times, half with an intensity of zero, and the subject is asked to say whether or not a (non-zero-intensity) flash occurred.

interesting if you are trying to measure some aspect of personality, but, at least for trying to understand *visual* processes, a somewhat different procedure is preferable.

Suppose you signal the occurrence of each flash with a click, and half the clicks are accompanied by a flash of some known intensity, but the other half (chosen at random) have no flash at all. The subject is not asked whether or not a flash was seen but rather whether or not, on each click, there *was* a flash, and the subject is required to give a yes or no answer even if it is purely a guess. (The subject can be trained a little before the actual data are collected, telling them whether or not each of their responses was correct.) Then the result will answer the question "How intense must a flash be in order that the information that an actual flash occurred will be detected by the subject?" The result of that procedure might look as plotted in figure 3.7. Note that the vertical axis in this plot is no longer "% seen" but rather "% correct."

Now another problem is revealed. The percentage of correct answers increases with intensity, but what percentage should be taken as indicating the threshold? The intensities at which the subject is correct 50 percent of the time are surely below what should be called the threshold, because the subject would be correct about 50 percent of the time even if the intensity was always zero—pure guesses. How about 51 percent? Maybe. If each intensity were presented, say, a hundred times during the study, the subject could easily have been purely guessing at that intensity and be correct 51 percent of the time, but if each intensity were presented a million times, it is very unlikely that a pure guess would be correct 51 percent of the time. So pick a number that provides the certainty that you want to have about whether or not the subject really saw the flashes. For instance, you might decide you want to be able to find the intensity for which there is only one chance in a hundred that the subject did not actually see the flash and was only guessing. Then get a statistician to compute the minimum number of times each intensity must be presented to get you there.

The procedure just described is similar to the one that was employed in the classic studies to measure dark-adapted sensitivity, but since that time a procedure has been developed that is much more efficient, that is, that requires the subject to make far fewer judgements. It is somewhat misleadingly called the staircase method. The basic procedure is this. Arbitrarily choose the intensity of the first flash. If the response to it is correct, reduce the intensity of the next flash; if it is incorrect, increase the intensity of the next flash. Continue the procedure until the intensity has reversed direction some predetermined number of times. Then the average of the last few intensities is taken as the threshold. That is the underlying process, but many improvements have been developed, such as lowering the intensity only after two responses to the same intensity have been correct, and beginning the procedure with large steps between intensity levels and reducing the size of the steps after some number of reversals. (As you can imagine, the staircase method generates a rather peculiar staircase, because the steps jump up and down. The procedure more closely resembles the method in chemistry and medicine called titration, which would be a better name for it.)

After the data collection procedure has been selected, there are still a lot more decisions to be made. The threshold will depend on the wavelength (color) of the stimulus, its size, how long each flash is, how much time there is between flashes, how large the test spot is, where the test spot is with respect to where the subject is looking, and so on. (Human vision is most sensitive to flashes delivered about 20 degrees away from the place that is being fixated, for instance if the flashed spot is one meter away from the eye and about a third of a meter to the side of the fixation target.) If you have no prior knowledge of how sensitivity is affected by those variables, you would just choose a convenient value for each and proceed. Then, if you wanted to investigate how the threshold is affected by one of the factors, for example, the duration of the flash, you could repeat the procedure for each of a number of flash durations.

The sensitivity of the dark-adapted human eye under optimal conditions has been measured by several researchers. It turns out that individual rod photoreceptors can signal the absorption of a single photon, and a subject will reliably detect a flash that causes the absorption of five or six photons close to each other on the retina within a tenth of a second. In the next chapter, some procedures will be described that allow you to experience this extraordinary sensitivity yourself.

THINGS TO THINK ABOUT

1. Why does a photon of long wavelength have such a low likelihood of being absorbed by a retinal pigment molecule?

2. A rod can be excited by the absorption of a single photon. Why, then, does it take five or six absorptions, all close together on the retina and within a tenth of a second, to reach the human visual threshold?

RELEVANT READING

An excellent discussion of the effects of light on photoreceptor pigment:
D.A. Baylor. 1987. "Photoreceptor Signals and Vision: Proctor Lecture." *Investigative Ophthalmology and Visual Science* 28: 34–49.

On the biochemistry of visual pigment regeneration (from straight to bent):
J.C. Saari. 2000. "Biochemistry of Visual Pigment Regeneration: The Friedenwald Lecture." *Investigative Ophthalmology and Visual Science* 41: 337–48.

CHAPTER FOUR

Seeing Things That Aren't There

What do you see when you close your eyes? If you ask that question, most people will give you a funny look, and then, if they answer at all, will say they don't see anything. They're sort of right—you don't see any *thing*. You don't see things like chairs or your cousin. But if you are carefully observant, you will recognize that you do have clear visual experiences when your eyes are closed, and after you've noticed a few, they will be very hard *not* to notice. Most of these experiences result from the receptor processes that were discussed in chapter 3.

Close your eyes (*not yet*) and pay attention to what you experience. It may take a minute or two, but you will see a lot. Fuzzy sparkles everywhere. Redness. Maybe faint lines. Exactly what you see depends on how bright the light is, what you were seeing right before you closed your eyes, and a lot of other factors, some of which have already been discussed and others that will be discussed later. If you don't notice anything, try putting your hand over your closed eyes. Unless you've been reading in the dark, you'll see a change in brightness, which might help you pay attention to your visual experience. *Close them now and observe what you see.*

When our eyes are open and the scene is lighted, some of the incident light is reflected from objects around us, and a small fraction of that light forms images of those objects on our retinas, as discussed in the chapter on optics, chapter 8. When our eyes are closed, our eyelids absorb some of the incident light, but eyelids are not opaque, so some of the light from the scene gets through to the retina. As will be clearer after you read chapter 8, all the mechanisms that enable vision are still working as usual, except for the optical mechanisms that form images. Our eyelids scatter light so thoroughly that images of the scene are completely blurred on the retina.

But, but, but—just because those visual mechanisms are there, it doesn't follow that you will see what you actually do see with your eyes closed. If the lids spread light evenly over your retinas, why don't you see a smooth lightness? If you see sparkles, for instance, something must have caused aspects of the visual system to be activated that cause nerve fibers to fire in the same ways they fire when you're looking at real sparkles with your eyes open.

Try this. Bring a pair of sunglasses (you might need them) and a piece of something opaque, like aluminum foil, that you can cover one eye with, go into a very dark room, and stay there for at least ten minutes. That will be enough time for a majority of the visual pigment molecules in your rods to assume their bent, light-sensitive state, as explained in chapter 3. (It's actually surprisingly difficult to make a room truly dark. If after ten minutes or so, you can still see things in the room, like a window or chair, it is not dark enough. Putting sunglasses on may help.)

As described in chapter 3, molecules in the bent state are not completely stable. Because all the components in molecules and atoms are constantly moving, occasionally a bent molecule will absorb enough energy from its surroundings to QM-change to its straightened state (recall that QM means quantum mechanical), triggering the events that lead to seeing. Since there are at least a million pigment molecules in each rod and rods are distributed over almost all the retina, in absolute darkness you will see flashes. Sometimes, for some people, flashes and similar visual events are initially very hard to see. That difficulty is not really a matter of the nature of the visual system, but is rather something about attention. Once you are tuned into observing visual experiences rather than looking for things in the world, it will be hard *not* to see flashes.

QM bleaching is not the only source of apparently spontaneous activity in the nervous system. Nerve fibers occasionally fire off impulses for no apparent reason (although it seems likely that all such activity is actually QM). However, there is excellent evidence that QM bleaching is very rare in the neural machinery sending signals from the photoreceptors to the brain in the dark-adapted rod visual system. A single rod can reliably signal the absorption of a single photon, and a dark-adapted human can sense the absorption of five or six photons if they fall near each other on the retina within about a tenth of a second. Therefore the other sources of "spontaneous" signals must be extremely rare in the dark-adapted rod system. If they were not rare, a lot more light would be required for us to distinguish between an actual flash and QM events.

If you sit in your very dark room for more than ten minutes or so, many, probably most, of the flashes you see with your eyes open will not be the result of QM bleaching of visual pigment molecules. They are much more likely to be actual absorptions of photons, because it is so difficult to make a room completely dark and because a dark-adapted human visual system has a reasonable probability of being excited by every photon that arrives at the retina. You can prove this by doing the following. While you are sitting in the dark watching flashes, cover your eyes with something opaque, for example aluminum foil, and observe the decrease, probably substantial, in the number of flashes. That is evidence that, in the absence of foil, many of the flashes are the results of photon absorptions. If you are a good observer, you will be able to tell that, when you cover just one eye with the foil while keeping the other open, the flashes will occur about half as often as when both eyes are open and neither is covered by foil. The fact that you still see flashes when both eyes are covered by foil is evidence that some are generated in your visual system, probably as the result of unbleached molecules QM-bleaching.

In a dark room with your eyes closed to reduce what little light there is, sparkles should be easy to see. Here's what's happening. To review what was discussed in previous chapters, the retina is a thin neural tissue that consists of several layers (seven or so, depending on how you count them). The layers farthest from the back of the eye, the layers that light hits first, are mostly transparent. Light passing through them hits a layer of receptors that are filled with molecules that absorb light: the visual pigment. When a photon of the right wavelength hits a visual pigment molecule, the molecule is likely to absorb the photon, and when it does, the molecule changes its shape.

If the pigment molecule hasn't absorbed a photon for a long time, the atoms that form it will be arranged in what is more or less a straight line bent near the middle. If a photon is absorbed, the molecule straightens out, isomerizes, which starts a cascade of events in the receptor, the end result of which is the triggering of the corresponding neuron. When the pigment molecule is straight, it is much less likely to absorb any photon that hits it. Then, during each second after it straightens, the molecule has a small probability of snapping back to its bent shape, ready to absorb another photon.

So why do we see sparkles in the dark? When a pigment molecule is sitting in the dark, it still has a small probability of QM straightening even without being hit by a photon. (That chance is *very* small. If you were watching a single molecule in the dark in a bent state, on average you would have to wait literally years before it straightened. But each receptor contains a million or more pigment molecules, any one of which can trigger the cascade that activates its nerve, so even though you would have to wait a very long time for any one particular molecule to straighten, you have to wait only a fraction of a second for at least a few of the millions of molecules in receptors to trigger a nerve impulse.)

When you've been in darkness for ten minutes or so, most of the pigment molecules are in their bent state, so your visual system is very sensitive. It's why you can see more after sitting in the dark movie theater for a while. It takes about forty minutes in darkness for almost all of the pigment molecules to get to their bent, sensitive state, the process called dark adaptation. But, in the dark, during each fraction of a second, each of the zillions of pigment molecules in your eye has a chance of straightening, so, each fraction of a second, a lot of them do straighten. That means they do the same thing as when they are hit by photons, so you see the same thing you would see when actual photons hit your retinas—call them sparkles. And once you know what to look for, you can see sparkles with your eyes closed in a lighted room too, partly because those same straightening events occur on top of the effects of actual light that gets through your lids, and partly because even apparently uniform light isn't really uniformly intense. The arrival of photons fluctuates over time and space, and you can see some of that variation.

When your eyes are fully dark-adapted, try this. Find a large region, for instance a wall, that is blank and illuminated very dimly. Looking at it carefully, you should see that its brightness seems grainy and fluctuating from inch to inch. Cover both eyes and then uncover one eye for a fraction of a second, cover it again, briefly uncover it again, and keep repeating. The graininess should become much more apparent. Here's what's happening. If you think of light as waves falling on a surface, reflecting from that surface, and finally falling on your retina, you might expect the light to be smoothly distributed, but when your eyes are detecting it, its particle-like properties are revealed. The photons detected by your retina are like drops of rain. The timing and place of the arrival of each photon is random, and, when you are dark adapted, your retina is so sensitive that it detects each photon or small group of photons, and you can actually see those detections and that randomness. If the reflected light level is high, there are so many detections that they all blend together and the region looks smoothly bright, but when the level is low enough, the randomness becomes visible.

There are two other kinds of things you can see with your eyes closed. One is very hard to see and the other is hard not to see. If you look for a second or more at a bright light and then close your eyes, it is hard not to see what is called an *afterimage*. First it will look like the bright light, called a *positive afterimage,* and then, after a few seconds (depending on how bright the light was and how long you looked at it), it will start changing color and brightness. If you then open your eyes (and you're not in the dark), that spot will look dark, called a *negative afterimage*.

DON'T EVER LOOK AT A VERY BRIGHT LIGHT, LIKE THE SUN, FOR MORE THAN A FEW SECONDS. IT CAN BURN YOUR RETINAS.

When you look at a bright light, a huge number of pigment molecules straighten and start cascades of events in their receptors. When you stop looking at the light, the chemical events in those cascades of events take a little while to dissipate, so you see a positive afterimage. But the process also causes a lot of pigment molecules to straighten and therefore to become non-reactive to light, so the region of the retina where the image of the light fell will become less sensitive than the surrounding regions and you will see a negative afterimage.

If you get really good at attending to what you see with your eyes closed, after a few minutes of trying, you may see some surprising things that are a lot harder to see, like a set of fine, dim, very low-contrast parallel lines, a precise spiral, or a regular pattern of circles. No one knows what causes these perceptions, but they are almost certainly generated in the brain rather than the retina, and it seems likely that they are sort of brain afterimages, images related in some perhaps symbolic way to things you were recently doing.

Most of the phenomena described in this chapter are not elicited by the retinal images of scenes but are generated within the visual system itself. In the next chapter, the conditions will be discussed under which major aspects of the retinal image, which you would expect to see easily, are almost always invisible. Some tricks will also be described that make them visible.

THINGS TO THINK ABOUT

I. Negative afterimages seem to disappear much more quickly than you might expect from the timing of dark adaptation. If they didn't disappear so quickly, how would they affect our visual experience?

2. In darkness, if you swing around a small bright light, like a sparkler on the fourth of July, the light seems to form a long streak. Why? Again in darkness, if you leave the bright light stationary but jump your line of sight from some distance on one side of it to the other, you will also see a streak. If you look from one side to the other of a light-emitting diode, like the ones used as indicator lights in most stereos, printers, and other electronic devices, you may also see a streak, but more likely you will see a train of separate bright dots. Why?

3. How would you find out whether the physiological events that cause negative afterimages are located in the retina or in the brain? What about positive afterimages?

CHAPTER FIVE

Not Seeing Things
That Are There

Although some visual experiences reveal events that originate within the physiology of the visual system itself, the opposite is also true; there are many conditions that might be expected to produce visual experiences but do not, and careful consideration of those experiences provides important clues leading to an understanding of normal vision.

Figure 5.1 is a photograph of the back of the eye as seen through the pupil, taken with a special camera. The darker lines that spread out over the picture are blood vessels. The lighter-colored oval to the left of the middle of the picture is the *optic disk*. (It is not properly called the *optical* disk.)

To give you an idea of the dimensions of the retina and retinal images with respect to the world, about ten images of the full moon could fit side by side within the optic disk. Arteries carry blood into the eye through the disk, and those arteries branch into smaller and smaller ones, as you can see. The blood then travels through very tiny vessels, capillaries, which are too small to see in the image, then into small and then larger veins and finally out of the eye again through the optic disk. The larger vessels are easy to see in figure 5.1. The darker region to the right of the optic disk and roughly the same size as the disk is the *macula*.

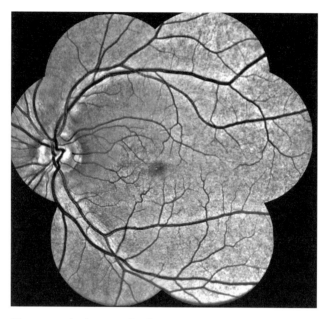

Figure 5.1. A photograph of the central region of a normal ocular fundus (the inside back surface of the eye). The region in the image has a diameter about one-third the whole diameter of the fundus.

At its center is a tiny region, the *fovea,* where the photoreceptors, cones, are packed very tightly together.

The capillaries dodge the fovea, as can be seen clearly in figure 5.2. The central gap in this photograph lies over the fovea. (About three images of the full moon would fit side by side in the gap.) The larger vessels are arteries, really arterioles, which bring oxygenated blood from the heart, and veins, that carry the blood away; and the narrowest channels, connecting the arteries to the veins, are capillaries. (There is a special technique, called adaptive optics, which provides the ability to photograph retinal features as small as capillaries in a living eye, but at least so far, it allows the imaging of only very small regions of the retina, so it doesn't reveal the overall structure of the vessels.)

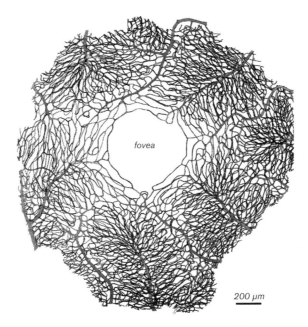

fovea

200 μm

Figure 5.2. The blood vessels over some of the same region with a diameter about one-eighth the diameter of the region in figure 5.1.

Another way to image the vascular structure of the retina of a living human is to inject a substance into the bloodstream that *fluoresces,* that is, glows, when it is illuminated with deep-blue light. Figure 5.3 is a photograph taken when the retina was illuminated with deep-blue light and just long enough after the injection that the substance has filled all the vessels. The deep blue light is blocked from getting to the image sensor. (This particular patient has a condition that causes the vessels near the fovea to leak blood, which is visible as fuzzy light patches.)

This whole blood-vessel structure lies in the layer of the retina that is right on the surface, delivering oxygen and nutrients to the layers of nerve tissue between the surface and the receptors. Therefore, the

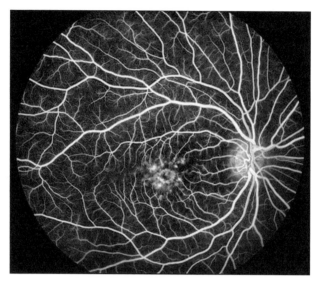

Figure 5.3. The blood vessels over about the same region as
in figure 5.1. Here the vessels in a living patient have been
filled with fluorescein, a substance that glows when
specially illuminated, so the vessels appear white.

vessels cast shadows on the layers beneath them, including the receptors, and the diameters of all of those vessels are larger than the diameters of the receptors. For instance, a typical vein where it enters the
optic disk is about twenty times as wide as a receptor. So the shadows of
the vessels are strong and ought to be easy to see. If you look at a blank
wall, for instance, the image of the wall that actually arrives at the
receptor layer will look like the picture in figure 5.2, or figure 5.3 with
the brightnesses inverted. That is, the vessels will be much darker than
their background. But what we see is vastly different from the image—
we don't see those great big, prominent features, the retinal blood vessel shadows. Why we don't see them is an amazing story, involving neural mechanisms that are fundamental to vision, but before we discuss
the reasons that we don't see blood vessel shadows, here's how to see
them.

On a day when there's a good stretch of blue sky (this also works if the sky is a smooth gray, though not quite as well), cover one eye and, with the other eye, stare at the sky. What do you see? You will probably say to yourself that you just see sky. But do you see anything moving? If you look very carefully, you will see that there's a lot of motion. If you don't see the motion, keep trying. It's hard to see at first, but once you do see it, seeing it again is a lot easier. Little spots move around in what look like random patterns at random times. Look still more carefully and you will see that while the spots move in apparently random paths, they actually follow the same random paths over and over again. Then pay attention to the timing. The motion is synchronized with your pulse!

What you are actually seeing is the movement of blood in your capillaries. The "random" paths are the paths of the capillaries. The blood flowing through the capillaries has many components. One component is corpuscles, which are dark red, and another is white cells, which are mostly transparent. The diameter of the capillaries is slightly smaller than the diameter of the corpuscles and white cells, so those cells don't flow smoothly, they push through the capillaries in single-file clumps, moving when the pressure of a pulse starts and stopping between pulses.

As a result of some neural mechanisms that will be discussed later, you can only see the blood when it's moving, so the visibility of the spots is synchronized with your pulse. If there were no white, that is, mostly transparent, cells, the corpuscles would solidly fill the capillaries, so your pulse would not produce changes in the shadows, and you wouldn't see motion. But the white cells, being transparent, let through little spots of light, and those spots are what you're actually seeing.

Now poke a tiny hole in a thin sheet of something that is fairly opaque, like a dark Post-it note, a magazine cover, or a sheet of aluminum foil, put the pinhole very close to your eye, and look at the sky through it (with the other eye covered). You probably won't see anything interesting at first, but try shifting the pinhole back and forth. First, you may see a dark spot right in the middle of where you're looking, and the spot will only be visible when the pinhole is moving. That

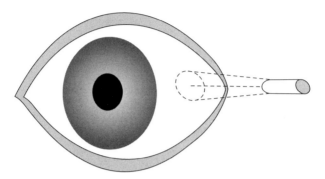

Figure 5.4. An eye being illuminated by a small spot of bright light on the white of the eye (the sclera). When the spot is moved around, the shadows of the larger retinal vessels become visible.

spot is a tiny clump of pigment, called macular pigment, that lies on the surface of the retina and so casts a shadow on the receptors. (People vary a lot in their amount of macular pigment. The more you have, the easier it is to see it when the pinhole moves.) The reason you see its shadow only when the pinhole is moving will be discussed later.

Now keep shifting the pinhole back and forth and pay close attention to what you see a little bit to the side of where you're looking. If you move the pinhole back and forth horizontally and look carefully enough, you will see wiggly vertical lines, and if you shift the pinhole up and down, you will see horizontal wiggly lines. If you are *really* observant, you may be able to tell that the wiggly lines you see follow the same paths as the moving spots you saw earlier. Through the moving pinhole, you are seeing the shadows of the blood vessels, and the reason that they only appear a little to the side of where you are looking should be evident from figure 5.2.

If you have a small bright flashlight, there is another, easier way to see the shadows of your larger retinal vessels. In a dimly lighted room, shine the light from a flashlight close to the white of your eye, off to the side of your eyeball, as sketched in figure 5.4. It is important that the spot of light, where it hits your eye, be fairly small.

You will probably just see a flare of light at first, but if you move the flashlight so that its light moves around on your eye, it will be hard not to see the shadows of the large blood vessels. (It's much harder to see the capillaries this way.) Since the light strikes the sclera, that is, hits the retina from the back, the blood vessels there do not lie between the incident light and the receptors, so you might expect that you wouldn't see their shadows. In fact, you don't see *those* shadows, you see shadows of the vessels on the other side of the retina. Some of the light has passed all the way through the layers of the eyeball where the light falls, and casts shadows on the receptors across the eyeball.

Blood-vessel shadows are there all the time. Why don't we see them all the time? That issue—and a closely related one, why we don't see afterimages much more frequently—are of fundamental importance and will be discussed extensively in chapter 11.

THINGS TO THINK ABOUT

1. The retinal capillaries are not visible in ordinary photographs of the retina, like figure 5.1, but they are visible in photographs like figure 5.3. Why?

2. To see the retina, the eye doctor or his camera must look through the optics of the eye, but those optics are not perfect, and they blur viewing just enough that the capillaries are not visible, although the larger vessels are. What's really happening when the image is "blurred"? And why do the capillaries become visible when they are lit up by the glow of fluorescein? Why are stars visible even though they are millions of miles away?

3. Seeing the shadows of your blood vessels as in figure 5.4 doesn't work if the spot of light falling on your sclera is large. The smaller the better. Explain why.

CHAPTER SIX

Brightness Constancy

A lot of things about vision, in fact probably *most* things about vision, seem perfectly natural and obvious until you think about them carefully. The phenomenon called *brightness constancy* is a good example that is evident in almost every scene we see.

On a typical day, the amount of light falling on every surface outside is hundreds of times greater than the amount falling on every surface inside. If an ordinary surface is not emitting its own light and doesn't get bleached by light, the amount it reflects will always be some constant percentage of the light falling on it. For instance, the black ink in this print reflects about 10 percent of the light falling on it (regardless of how much light falls on it) and the white paper reflects about 80 percent of the incident light. Let's say the amount of incident light falling on this page when it is inside is 1,000 somethings, for instance 1,000 photons per second per square millimeter. Then, inside, the ink reflects 100 somethings per second and the paper reflects 800. During daytime, the amount of light outside can easily be 100 times the amount inside, and it is often a lot more intense than that. If you take this book outside and the amount of light falling on the book is 100 times greater, then the ink will reflect 10,000 somethings and the paper 80,000. That is, the *ink* outside reflects $10,000/800 = 12.5$ times as much light as the *paper* reflects

Figure 6.1. A simple pattern to illustrate that the perceived brightnesses in a scene change very little even when the intensities of the light reflected from the various parts of the scene change strongly.

inside. That's the physics of it. But the ink doesn't even come close to looking brighter outside than the paper does inside. In fact, so long as the light isn't extremely dim or extremely bright, the paper and ink look pretty much the same inside as they do outside. In general, so long as the light isn't extremely dim or bright, all ordinary things look about the same inside or outside. The brightnesses of things appear fairly constant in spite of changes in illumination, and this phenomenon is called brightness constancy (or, sometimes, lightness constancy).

When you move this picture (figure 6.1) so that the amount of light falling on it changes, its appearance hardly changes. When you take something from inside to outside, the *thing* doesn't change, so it seems as though it should be no surprise that it *looks* the same. But as soon as you know a little about the physics of light, constancy becomes a puzzle. We see things as the things themselves "are," instead of responding to the only information that actually informs us about things, the light that's reflected from them. Is constancy an illusion? Or an anti-illusion?

Many people who study visual perception have "explained" brightness constancy by saying that the brain knows or has learned that the thing itself doesn't change when you take it outside, so that's the way you see it. That's not an explanation, it just says that the puzzle happens in the brain, but doesn't say how it happens. And it's probably not even true that the mechanisms that perform this trick are in the brain. There are two main mechanisms, and they are in the retina. There is good scientific evidence about these neural mechanisms. Each of them is simple, although each requires a lot of explaining, and they combine in an interesting way to produce brightness constancy.

The logic underlying the understanding of constancy and many related phenomena is as follows. If two things look identical, then it must be true that somewhere in the visual system, the neural events corresponding to those two things are identical. (It almost follows that if two sets of neural events, for example, the signals that are sent from the retina from two scenes, are identical, then the two scenes will look identical. The "almost" is because it is possible that, somewhere in the brain, there might be knowledge about the scene that could affect the signals coming from the retina after they arrive in the brain.)

One of the mechanisms that underlies constancy has to do with the relationship between the rate at which each receptor is absorbing photons and the strength of the signal that the receptor delivers to its associated neural circuits. This has been described earlier, in chapter 3, with respect to a different aspect of vision, and will be discussed again here.

It seems logical that if twice as many photons are being absorbed every second, a receptor will deliver twice as strong a signal. That relationship is illustrated in figure 6.2.

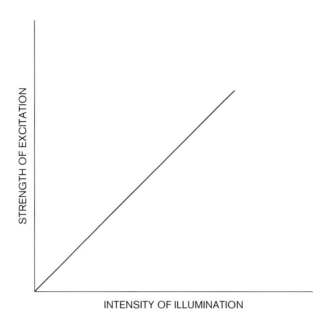

Figure 6.2. A hypothetical linear relationship between the intensity of illumination on a receptor and the strength of the excitation it produces.

But that idea is wrong. The first condition where it is clearly wrong is when the light level is very low. When the light level is zero, that idea requires that the neural output will also be zero, but QM bleaching still goes on, so the output strength never goes to zero, and we still see things in the dark.

That idea is also wrong for another reason. When a pigment molecule has absorbed a photon and is in its straightened, bleached state, it won't absorb another photon, and it won't return to its bent, ready-to-absorb-a-photon state for about seven minutes on average for a rod and one minute for a cone. Therefore, as the incident light level increases, more and more pigment molecules in a receptor will be in their unabsorbing, bleached state. Fewer and fewer will be ready to absorb a photon. So as the light intensity increases, the receptor output will not increase as fast as it would if the molecules didn't bleach. The curve

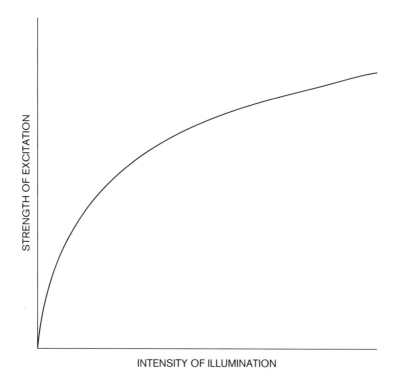

Figure 6.3. A logarithmic relationship between the intensity of light falling on a region of the retina and the corresponding strength of neural response. This relationship would produce perfect brightness constancy.

will look more like the one in figure 6.3. That graph shows one particular relationship, in which the output is proportional to what is called the logarithm of the input.

If the relationship were like that in figure 6.2, then if the intensity were doubled, the resulting excitation would also double; but if the relationship is logarithmic, like the one in figure 6.3, each time the intensity doubles, the excitation increases by some fixed amount. For example, if the intensity is, say, 10, and that produces a strength of excitation of, say, 1, then if the intensity is doubled, that produces an intensity of 1.3 (the logarithm of 20), and if the intensity is doubled again, the

Figure 6.4. The same pattern as in figure 6.1, repeated here
for convenience.

resulting excitation will be 1.6 (the logarithm of 40). (Those are logarithms with a base of 10, but the arguments apply regardless of the particular base.) Each time the intensity is doubled, the excitation does not
double, it increases by a fixed amount, 0.3 in this example. The special
thing about that logarithmic relationship is in the way it relates vision
to the physics of light.

Look at the pattern in figure 6.1 again, repeated as figure 6.4. The
annulus is printed so that it reflects 25 percent of the incident light and
the disk reflects 75 percent, three times as much. Suppose the light
intensity falling on the whole pattern is 100 photons per second per
square millimeter (that is extremely unrealistic—the intensity might
well be millions of times higher—but let's pick numbers that are
easier to use). Then each square millimeter in the annulus will reflect

25 photons toward your eye, and in the disk 75 photons, three times as much. If the visual system behaved like the one in figure 6.2, the excitation from the annulus might be 25 and from the disk, 75, so the difference between the neural signals at the border between the disk and annulus would be 50.

Now suppose you look at the pattern during the day outside, where the incident light level is 100 times higher, 10,000 photons. The annulus will reflect 2,500 photons, and the disk 7,500. If the system behaves like the one in figure 6.2, the difference at the border between the disk and the annulus will now be 5,000.

But consider what happens if the system behaves like the one in figure 6.3, the logarithmic relationship. Indoors, the annulus output will be 25 and the disk output will be 75, for a ratio of 3. And under the higher illumination outside, the annulus output will be 2,500 and the disk output 7,500, so the ratio will again be 3—exactly the same as it was indoors. And since the ratio is the same, when the relationship is logarithmic, the *difference* in the response strength, that is, the change in signal at the edges, will be the same. It will depend on the *relative* amounts of light reflected from different places in the pattern, and the relative amounts don't change when the intensity of illumination changes. A logarithmic relationship between light intensity and strength of excitation will produce relationships in excitations among different regions of the retina that are the same as the relationships among the physical properties of the object being looked at. That is, the patterns of excitation in the visual system would correspond not to the light intensities in the scene but to the physical properties of the objects themselves.

As was mentioned in chapter 3 and will be discussed extensively in chapter 7, effects of the rates of bleaching and unbleaching may generate a relationship between intensity and receptor output that is close to a logarithmic one. A theory regarding the differences in the actions of the visual system under different illumination intensities, called IDS (intensity-dependent summation), also generates a logarithmic relationship. The IDS theory proposes that when a receptor is illuminated, it spreads the resulting excitation over a neighboring area in such a way that the total amount of excitation is constant regardless of the intensity of illumination, but if the intensity decreases the excitation spreads over a larger region of the retina and the strength of excitation at each point decreases. The IDS theory was developed to explain the fact that visual acuity improves strongly as the intensity of light reflected from the scene increases, but it also inherently produces a logarithmic relationship between the intensity of light falling on receptors and the strength of their outputs, a relationship that produces brightness constancy.

In chapter 11, strong evidence is presented that the apparent lightness of any uniform region, like the disk in figure 6.4, does not depend on the amount of light it reflects but only on the changes in intensity at the borders in the retinal images of the region. Now if we combine the two mechanisms—that the brightness of each uniform region in a scene depends only on its borders and that the output of each receptor is proportional not to the light intensity on the retina but to the logarithm of that light intensity—then when we look at any scene, the pattern of outputs from the retina will be the same regardless of the intensity of the light falling on the scene, that is, we will have brightness constancy. (The actual relationship between light level and receptor output is not exactly the same as the one plotted in figure 6.3, but it is close. And brightness constancy does not hold exactly, but it is close.)

The evidence for the logarithmic relationship between light level and visual response that is probably best known among people studying vision is called Weber's law. Present a subject with a large disk of light at some intensity, flash a small spot on top of it to add a little more light there, and adjust the amount of added light so that it is just intense enough that the subject can tell that the added flash occurred. It turns out that for almost the entire range of light intensities over which the visual system operates, the "threshold" amount of added light is a fixed fraction of the background light. Put another way, a just-detectable increment is one that increases the light level by some fixed percentage. That percentage depends on the overall conditions, like the sizes of the spots, but, for example, if a flash adding 2 percent of the background light to a dim background is just barely detectable, an increment of 2 percent of the background light added to an intense background will also be just barely detectable. That the threshold increment in intensity is a fixed percentage of the background intensity could only happen if the excitation produced by the absorption of photons is proportional to the logarithm of the intensity.

If you move an object from inside to outside, its brightness won't change much, and its color won't change much either. The latter phenomenon is called *color constancy*. Why you might expect the color to change and why it doesn't are closely related to the explanation of brightness constancy, because, as explained in the discussion of color vision in chapter 10, the colors we see depend on the *ratios* of the excitations of the different kinds of cones in our eyes.

THINGS TO THINK ABOUT

1. Can you think of any scenes (other than ones that are extremely dark or extremely bright) in which brightness constancy does not hold?

2. Would you call brightness constancy an illusion? Or maybe an anti-illusion?

RELEVANT READING

T. N. Cornsweet and J. I. Yellott. 1985. "Intensity-Dependent Spatial Summation." *Journal of the Optical Society of America A* 2: 1769–86.

CHAPTER SEVEN

Why the Rate of Unbleaching Is Important

The material in this chapter is complicated but give it a try.

Chapter 3 contained a detailed discussion of the very first physiological events that affect vision. Each photoreceptor includes a membrane and a mechanism that continuously pumps ions, generating a voltage across the membrane. Visual pigment molecules are imbedded in holes in the membrane and partially plug those holes, allowing some current to flow. When a pigment molecule absorbs a photon, the molecule changes its shape, and in effect it swells, reducing the amount of current that can flow through the hole it is imbedded in.

So the very first effect of the absorption of light is to *decrease* the current. That current *inhibits* a neuron that is directly connected to it, and the inhibited neuron controls another neuron that in turn produces an increase in the excitation of an optic nerve fiber. The optic nerve fiber conducts signals, impulses, to the brain. By that apparently indirect route, when a photon is absorbed, less current flows through the membrane, which reduces the inhibition, so the corresponding optic nerve fiber fires more strongly. That is the sort of a roundabout way that has evolved to cause an increase in the activity of the optic nerve when the light increases. (Note that the nerve cells just referred to are not the only cells in the retina that are driven by receptors and ultimately drive optic nerve fibers. Other nerve cells in the various layers of the retina mediate interactions among neighboring regions. Some of those actions will be discussed in chapter ii.)

When a pigment molecule changes its shape, when it isomerizes, it not only tends to plug up the hole it is imbedded in; its change in shape is also such that it no longer can absorb a photon. It "bleaches." Then, after some time in its bleached state, it will return to its original shape—it will "unbleach" and once again become sensitive to light. Those are the events that control the first steps in vision. All the subsequent processes depend on the bleaching and unbleaching of visual pigment. The way those processes change over time has profound effects on what we see, and they can be different from what we might expect, so they will be discussed at some length in this chapter.

When a pigment molecule plugs a hole in the membrane it is imbedded in, the hole stays plugged for, on average, about one minute for cones and seven for rods. However, the reduction in the flow of current through the hole does not continue for that whole length of time. Instead, as a result of a complicated series of electrochemical interactions in the neural tissue between the receptor and the corresponding optic nerve fiber, the reduction in current lasts only for a tenth of a second or so. Therefore, in effect, each absorption of a photon causes a brief reduction in current, which produces a brief increase in the excitation of the optic nerve fiber. When a series of absorptions occur in a photoreceptor close together in time, their effects simply add together. The overall effect is that the excitation of the optic nerve fiber is related not to the total number of bleached molecules but rather to the *rate* at which molecules bleach.

Our vision is functional over a limited range of illumination intensities. Suppose you've been looking for a minute or longer at a large computer screen that has no pattern on it but is uniformly illuminated at a level that, for example, causes 100 photons to fall on each square millimeter of your retina per second. Then for a few seconds the uniform field is replaced by an ordinary scene, for instance a landscape, that reflects varying intensities, so that different regions of the retinal image receive different intensities ranging from, say, 1 to 2,000 photons per square millimeter per second. Then the scene is replaced by a uniform field at 100 again. While the scene is on, detail will not be visible in any of the regions of the scene delivering fewer than about 10 photons per second per square millimeter—those regions will appear uniformly dark—and all regions delivering more than about 1,000 photons will appear uniformly bright, so that the range of intensities over which you will be able to see things is about 10 to 1,000, a ratio of 1 to 100. (Those intensity numbers, photons per second per square millimeter, are surely lower than would be representative of an actual scene. They are intended only to make the arithmetic easier to follow.)

Now, if that procedure is repeated but the screen is initially set to deliver 100 times as many photons per second per square millimeter, that is, 10,000 photons, as a uniform field, and all the intensities in the scene are also multiplied by 100, your visual system will still provide vision over a range of about 1 to 100, but that range will be shifted upward on the overall range by about 100-fold, so that all regions delivering fewer than 1,000 photons will appear uniformly dark and all regions delivering more than 100,000 will appear equally bright. This shift in the place on the overall range of visible brightnesses is partly the result of the fact that, as the intensity increases, the proportion of bleached, insensitive visual pigment molecules increases, and it may also be partly a consequence of a not-yet-understood reorganization of the connections among the neurons that deliver signals to the brain.

When we look at a scene, say of a deer in the middle of the road, an image of it is formed on our retinas. Since the scene contains regions that reflect different amounts of light, corresponding regions on the retinas are illuminated by different intensities, and they respond with different strengths that correspond to the light intensities in the scene. Therefore we are able to distinguish the various features of the scene—the pattern of the deer's hide, the shapes of the trees, the texture of the road.

The strength of excitation of optic nerve fibers, and the resulting brightness of the corresponding part of the scene, depends on the rate of bleaching of unbleached pigment molecules. For instance, if there's a puddle on the road that reflects sunlight toward our eyes, the corresponding spots on our retinas will undergo an increased rate of bleaching, the nerve fibers will send stronger signals from those spots, and the puddle will look bright. If pigment molecules bleached when they absorbed photons but did not unbleach, then after a few seconds in light, all the pigment molecules would be bleached and therefore unable to absorb more light. Because molecules do bleach when they absorb photons, having vision requires that they also unbleach. If a molecule is in the bleached state, there is some probability that it will isomerize back to its sensitive state, that is, unbleach, in each second. The higher the rate of unbleaching, the sooner any bleached molecule will unbleach and therefore the sooner our eyes will regain sensitivity.

Figure 7.1 shows how the rate of bleaching changes as a function of the time after the light was turned on, for five different illumination levels. (The receptor was in darkness for a long time before the light was turned on.) The higher the intensity of the light, the faster the pigment bleaches, so the stronger the initial excitation evoked by the photoreceptors. Note that the higher-intensity curves fall so fast, that is, the pigment bleaches so rapidly, that they actually cross the lower-intensity curves. That suggests that if a very intensely illuminated region were presented next to an even more intensely illuminated region, the brightnesses would actually be reversed for a few seconds, and that is what actually happens. Because the quantities on both the horizontal and vertical axes in this graph depend on other factors, such as the particular visual pigment being plotted, the density of pigment, and so on, no numbers are attached to the scales, but each division on the horizontal axis typically represents only a second or two.

For a fixed rate of unbleaching and at high intensities, after leveling off, the rate of bleaching becomes about the same regardless of the intensity. Under those conditions, there are so many photons arriving

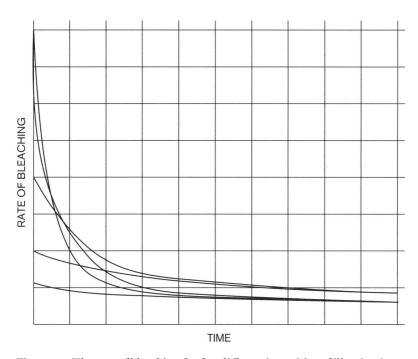

Figure 7.1. The rate of bleaching for five different intensities of illumination.

that as soon a bleached molecule unbleaches it is struck by another photon, so the rate of bleaching depends almost entirely on the rate of unbleaching. At even higher intensities and high rates of unbleaching, when the illumination first turns on, essentially all the pigment is immediately bleached, resulting in almost no new bleaching until pigment becomes unbleached, and what follows is an oscillation in the rate of bleaching, as shown in figure 7.2. If the conditions for this oscillation occur, that is, if you are dark-adapted and an extremely bright light is suddenly turned on, the brightness might seem to fluctuate for the first fraction of a second. (The lowest two curves in figure 7.2 are the same as the lower two curves in figure 7.1, but with a different scaling of the vertical axis.)

If unbleaching did not happen, the curves for all intensities of light would continue to fall until all of the pigment was bleached. That is,

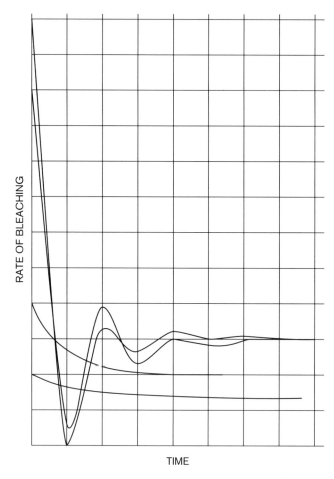

Figure 7.2. The rate of bleaching for higher intensities.

the curves for all intensities would end up with the same rate of bleaching, zero molecules bleached per second. Curves for higher intensities would fall faster and would reach total bleaching sooner, but after a second or two, all intensities would result in zero bleaching. Differences in intensity would not produce differences in signals sent up the optic nerve. The deer, the road, and the trees would be indistinguishable, as if the whole scene were in complete darkness. *Unbleaching is crucial.*

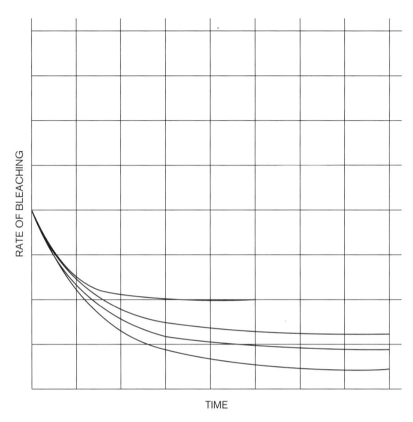

Figure 7.3. The rate of bleaching for four different rates of unbleaching.

Figure 7.3 illustrates, for a fixed intensity, how the rate of bleaching changes for different rates of unbleaching. During each second that a bleached molecule sits in the receptor, there is some probability that it will unbleach, and that probability depends on the nature of the molecule's surroundings. The curves in figures 7.3 represent different particular probabilities, that is, some particular rates of unbleaching. The top curve represents the change over time in the rate at which molecules bleach for a high rate of unbleaching, and each of the successively lower curves represents a rate of unbleaching that is half that of the curve above it.

If the chemical constituents that surround the pigment were different, the probabilities would be different, and the curves would change.
For example, as illustrated in figure 7.3, if the surrounding chemicals
caused a bleached molecule to unbleach sooner, the proportion of the
molecules that are in the bleached state would decrease, and the curve
would shift upward. If something happened to change the chemistry in
your eyes so that the rate of unbleaching were suddenly increased, the
strengths of all the neural signals emerging from your eyes would
increase, so it would look as if the sun suddenly got brighter.

It is entertaining to analyze the environmental forces that have
shaped evolution, especially since it is almost always impossible to prove
or disprove any relevant hypothesis. So the following is a speculation
about the conditions that gave rise to the properties of the human visual
system that govern the range of light intensities over which we have useful vision.

As a basis for this speculation, here are some things that must be
true of the responses of the retina.

- There is a maximum rate at which neurons can fire impulses.
  (Some neurons in the human body can fire up to about 1,000
  impulses per second, but the maximum rate for neurons in the
  human visual system is unknown, because, at least with present
  technology, there is no way to measure it without injury to the
  visual system.)
- The act of seeing usefully involves not the response to a light level
  but rather the difference in responses to differences in light levels
  in different places (or a change in light level at a given place).
- After light has been falling on receptors for some time, so that
  the change in output that began when the light was first turned
  on is complete:
- If the light is of very low intensity, the receptor output will be
  directly proportional to the intensity of the light. The reason is
  that, at low intensities, very little visual pigment is in the

bleached state, so each new photon that arrives has an essentially equal probability of being absorbed and bleaching a molecule.

· At very high intensities, the receptor output depends only on the rate of *unbleaching* of pigment molecules. When the intensity is very high, almost all of the pigment molecules are in the bleached state, so most of the arriving photons are not absorbed. But as soon as a molecule unbleaches, it is likely to be struck by another photon, so the rate of bleaching will equal the rate of unbleaching.

As explained earlier, the higher the rate at which pigment molecules are bleached, the weaker is the current output by a receptor, and thus the weaker the *inhibition* acting on the corresponding optic nerve; and the result is that the higher the rate of bleaching, the stronger is the signal sent up the optic nerve. The rate of bleaching of molecules at any time determines the strength of excitation of the optic nerve fiber at that time.

The curves in figures 7.1 and 7.2 represent the time course of changes in the rate of bleaching of molecules for different intensities. The rate of firing of the corresponding optic nerve fiber will increase as the rate of bleaching increases, so the rate of firing will also increase when the intensity increases. But there is a limit to how fast a nerve can fire impulses.

Figure 7.4 shows the relationships between the intensity of light falling on the retina (on the horizontal axis) and the resulting rate of bleaching of visual pigment molecules *after the light level has been constant* for enough time that the corresponding curves, like those in figures 7.1 and 7.2, have flattened out (usually a fraction of a second). Each curve in figure 7.4 represents the rate of bleaching of pigment molecules for a particular probability or rate of unbleaching, and, as will be explained, illustrates the effect of the rate of unbleaching on the range of light intensities over which we have useful vision. The leftmost curve represents a very low rate of unbleaching, that is, when a molecule is in the bleached state it is likely to take a long time before it unbleaches, and each successive curve to the right represents a higher rate of unbleaching.

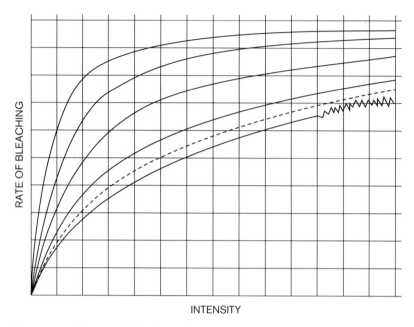

Figure 7.4. The rate of bleaching after it has leveled off, for five rates of unbleaching (solid curves). The dashed curve represents a logarithmic relationship.

The rightmost curve thus represents a high rate of unbleaching. When both the rate of unbleaching and the intensity are high, the rate of bleaching begins to oscillate, as shown in figure 7.2, and depending on the intensity and rate of unbleaching, those oscillations do not die out over time; they can continue indefinitely, as indicated in figure 7.4. This is true for all curves for which both the intensity and the rate of unbleaching are high. It seems likely that evolutionary forces would set the rate of unbleaching to a value low enough that this instability would not occur under illumination levels that we encounter on Earth. If instability did occur in some range of intensities, places in the scene producing those intensities on our retinas would appear to flicker, delivering signals to our brains that would be inconsistent with the actual state of the world. (Have you ever noticed a slight occasional flickering way off in your peripheral vision when the light is dim? When the illumination seems dim but there is enough light that things are still easily visible, the cones are stimulated at a low level but the rods are strongly stimulated, so they are near the level where, in figure 7.4, the response is leveling off. Maybe that flicker is a manifestation of the oscillations that occur at high light levels—high for rods, that is.)

The dashed curve in figure 7.4 is a plot of the relationship between intensity and the logarithm of intensity, that is, the condition that would provide many advantages, such as brightness constancy and Weber's law, as discussed in chapter 6. The curve just above the dashed line is closest in shape to the logarithmic relationship, so the rate of unbleaching it represents provides the greatest range of intensities over which changes in light level provide strong changes in receptor output without instabilities and also a large range over which the relationship is approximately logarithmic.

One more factor may have influenced the evolution of the unbleaching rate. As the rate of bleaching increases, that is, as the curves rise, the firing rate of the corresponding optic nerve fiber will increase; but there is a maximum firing rate, which could be represented as a horizontal line at some height in figure 7.3. (Quantitative data that would indicate the actual height of such a line in the figure are not available, so that line is not drawn.) Evolution may have acted to produce as high an unbleaching rate as possible while still keeping the bleaching below one that would cause the firing rate to reach its maximum. That would provide the greatest range of intensities over which vision can operate.

Of course this is speculation. There are surely other ways to explain the factors that have shaped the evolution of the range of intensities over which our visual system can function, but the argument presented in relationship to figure 7.3 might be the correct one and is an example of the kinds of theories that can be constructed.

The rods in our retinas allow us to see usefully over the range of light levels that occur at night. The rate of unbleaching in the cone system is appreciably faster than in the rods, and provides cone-mediated vision with a useful intensity range that matches almost all of the intensities present on Earth in daylight. That the range for cones begins at a light level near the top of the rod range and extends to much higher levels is probably due to the fact that, while a rod requires the absorption of only one photon to send a signal, cones require the absorption of more than one. As a result, we have vision that functions over an enormous range of illumination levels. The only natural source of light levels at the retina that exceed the range of cone vision is a direct look at the sun. Although the intensities of light radiating from the sun differ greatly from place to place on its surface, those levels are mostly above the maximum of the intensity range, so the sun looks uniformly bright.

DON'T CHECK THAT STATEMENT OUT! STARING AT THE SUN CAN BURN YOUR RETINAS.

There are a very few people whose retinas contain only rods, no cones. The range of intensities over which their rods respond extends into the daylight range, but at most daylight levels, they see only glare. The scene looks uniformly bright and featureless. There are also people whose retinas contain no rods. Those people are sometimes referred to as night-blind.

For people with normal retinas, there is a range of illumination levels between moonlight and daylight in which both rods and cones contribute to vision, but at lower levels the cones are not functional, as indicated by the absence of color in our view of nighttime scenes, and at typical daylight levels, the signals from rods do not contribute to vision. (In daylight, rods probably produce what would appear as a field of almost uniform brightness superimposed on the varying signal patterns from cones, and, as explained in chapter II, a neural network in the normal visual system suppresses signals from uniform fields, that is, scenes that have only very gradual or no intensity gradients.)

In discussions about vision, the unbleaching of visual pigment is almost always referred to in relation to the process called dark adaptation, the way that our sensitivity to light slowly increases if we are in darkness. But without unbleaching, we would not be able to see at all, and the ways that unbleaching powerfully affects the range of intensities over which we can see is rarely if ever mentioned. In this chapter, the critically important effects of unbleaching and of differing rates of unbleaching have been examined and analyzed.

When we look at a scene, the optics of our eyes produce, on our retinas, tiny replicas of the distribution of light intensities and wavelengths in the scene, and the neural elements in our retinas respond, providing us with some of the information in the scene. In the following chapters, the processes by which retinal images are formed will be analyzed, and some of the practical consequences of those processes will be discussed.

THINGS TO THINK ABOUT

1. What good do sunglasses do?
2. After you've been in darkness for a while, two patches of light, next to each other, are suddenly turned on, one very intense and the other even more intense. How do the relative brightnesses of the two patches appear as a function of the time after onset?
3. Have you ever seen an area so bright that part of it looks dark? How could that happen?
4. If you had an insufficiency of some vitamin that was required for unbleaching to occur, how would your vision be affected?

RELEVANT READING

T.N. Cornsweet. 1962. "Changes in the Appearance of Stimuli of Very High Luminance." *Psychological Review* 69: 257–73.

CHAPTER EIGHT

A Little Optics

So far, the discussion has primarily been about the effects of light on the retina, but a critical step in the visual process involves transferring the spatial information in the scene into the eye, that is, producing a copy of the spatial distribution of light in the scene as a spatial distribution of light on the retina. To understand that process and its visual consequences, a short discussion of optics is needed. Although this discussion covers only a small fraction of optical phenomena, it does cover the general characteristics of optics that you need in order to understand the formation of retinal images and also to understand some of the procedures that eye practitioners routinely perform.

Here are some terms that will be used in this discussion and that are important to clarify. First, the term *point* refers to a geometrical concept. It is not a thing but rather a location, an infinitesimally small area. The term *source* refers to something that emits photons, a generator of light, like the sun or a star or a lightbulb. The important term *point source* refers to a source that appears to be extremely small.

The concept of a point source is actually more complicated that it first seems, and requires further explanation. As will be discussed extensively in this chapter, if photons emitted from a very small source far away pass through a typical lens, the lens will cause the paths of those photons to converge, and the light distribution in the plane where they converge most closely is called the *image* of the source. (Images of sources larger than points will also be discussed, but their description will be based on the discussion of point sources.)

Because of the wave-like nature of light, even if the source is infinitesimal and the lens has the best possible shape, the photons in the image won't all converge to one point. They will spread out over a small but finite area. (The reasons why that spread occurs will be explained later in the chapter.) As will also be explained, if an object moves farther away from the lens, its image will become smaller. Therefore, the image of a large source very far away can become so small that it is indistinguishable from the image of a very tiny source that is near. Stars are good examples. Their images, even those formed by powerful telescopes, are no larger than images of extremely tiny sources. Given all that, the term *point source* means any source of light whose image cannot be distinguished from the image of an infinitesimally small source. (The image of one point source might be *brighter* than the image of another—that is, there might be more photons in the image of one point source than another—but the areas over which the photons arrive will be equal.)

As mentioned earlier, light can be best described under some conditions as a stream of particles of energy and under other conditions as a set of waves. Thinking of light as a stream of particles, as will be done here initially, makes the general properties of image formation easier to grasp but leads to inaccuracies in detail. The bending of paths of light, the basis of image formation, is fundamentally a process involving the wave-like properties of light, and that process will be discussed as well.

The speed of light in a vacuum is a famous constant, about 186,000 miles (about 300,000 kilometers) per second. However, if light enters a transparent medium like glass, it slows down by an amount that depends on the particular medium. The speed in air is only very slightly less than in a vacuum. Most kinds of glass slow it down to about two-thirds as fast, corneal tissue to about three-quarters as fast. Its speed depends

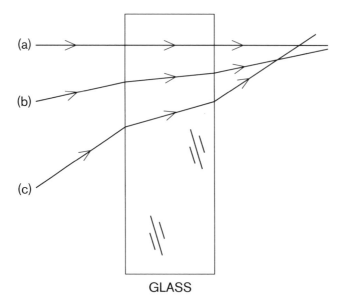

Figure 8.1. Rays passing through a slab of glass. The larger the angle between the ray and the perpendicular to the surface of the glass, the greater the angle through which the ray is bent.

on the medium it is traveling through, so it if passes from glass back to air, it goes back to almost full speed.

If you could watch a photon in a beam of light, it would appear to travel along some path, and that path is called a *ray*. The ray labeled (a) in figure 8.1 travels left to right, first through air, and then hits the surface of the glass at an angle perpendicular to the surface. The photon will slow down when entering the glass, but because the ray is perpendicular to the surface, the path of the photon will not be bent, or probably it is better to say that the ray will be bent through an angle of zero degrees. However, if the ray hits the glass at an angle, when it enters the glass and slows down it will bend toward the perpendicular, like the rays labeled (b) and (c). The bigger the angle between the ray and the perpendicular to the surface, the more the ray is bent; and the more the glass slows the photon down, the more its path bends. Then, when the ray passes through the surface of the glass and back to air, it regains its original speed; but because the two surfaces of the glass are parallel, the angles are reversed, so it bends back to its original direction of travel. Physicists call this bending of the rays *refraction*. (Just to add to the confusion, the same term is used by eye care practitioners to refer to the process of finding a patient's prescription for eyeglasses or contact lenses. That process will be discussed in chapter 9.)

Using rays to represent the paths of photons does indicate, approximately, how light behaves when it encounters media that cause it to change speed, and the effects of refraction can be illustrated easily using rays, but *why* refraction occurs cannot be explained in terms of rays. Refraction is fundamentally a consequence of the wave-like properties of light. The drawing in figure 8.2, which is often used as an explanation of refraction, illustrates why it must be understood in terms of a wave-like rather than a particle-like description of light. Figure 8.2 is a good example of shallow thinking leading to a wrong answer. The men are marching from a grassy field into mud, and they slow down when they enter the mud. It is said that, because they slow down, they change their direction of travel. But why should the direction of travel of each individual man change? If there were only one lone man, why would he change direction? He would just keep walking straight—unless he were marching among rows of men, maybe soldiers, and had been instructed to change direction if necessary in such a way that the line formed by those in his row stayed perpendicular to the direction of travel. That is, he would only change his direction if he had neighbors and if he used continuous information about where they were. So if he does change direction, he cannot be behaving as an individual, separate particle would. Instead, he and the others must be spreading information about themselves to their neighbors. That is, the group is behaving like a wave. Refraction is an example of the wave-like properties of light.

But rays are a relatively easy tool with which to illustrate the general *results* of refraction in a way that is sufficient to provide a rough

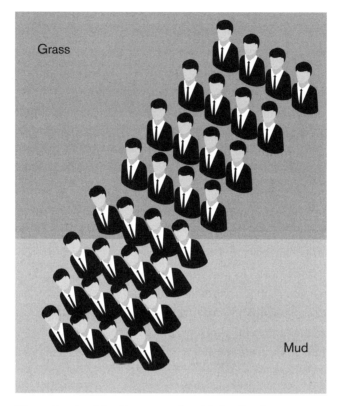

Figure 8.2. A misleading way to "explain" refraction.

understanding of retinal image formation and of the procedures that eye doctors perform, so rays will be used as a tool in this chapter. Thinking of light in terms of waves is a way of understanding *why* refraction occurs, and provides a more accurate description of how light behaves before it is actually detected. (As it is being detected, its behavior is better understood in terms of particles of energy, photons.)

Figure 8.3 illustrates exactly the same optical process as in figure 8.1, refraction, except that the glass is in the shape of a prism. There are only three rays drawn in figure 8.3 for each prism, but they are a representative sample of a huge number of rays, paths of photons, all heading for the prism. Those rays are all parallel in the drawing, so they all

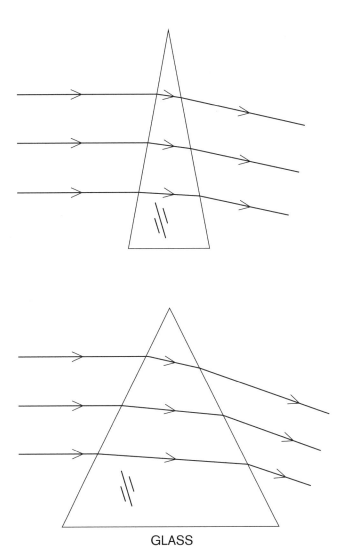

Figure 8.3. Groups of rays passing through prisms, the same process as illustrated in figure 8.1.

strike the surfaces of the glass at the same angle and undergo the same amount of bending.

The rays represent the paths of photons. If the source of those photons were a tiny bright point in air or a vacuum, the photons would travel off from it along straight paths in all directions. That is, the rays would radiate out in straight lines in all directions. So if the prism were near the source, the rays striking it would be diverging. However, if the rays arriving at the prism are essentially parallel, as they are in figure 8.3, they must represent photons coming from a point source very far away. The actions of parallel rays are somewhat easier to understand, so for this and some of the figures that follow, the source will be assumed to be a tiny bright point a long distance away, a point source.

In figure 8.3, the rays that are drawn are parallel. Because the angles between the rays and the surfaces of the glass in the lower prism are larger than in the upper prism, the rays are bent more strongly. (Different wavelengths are slowed by different amounts in glass, and the degree to which the angle of a ray bends at a surface depends on the amount of slowing. Therefore, if the light passing through a prism contains different wavelengths, the different wavelengths will be bent through different angles as they enter and exit the glass. Because sunlight contains a wide range of wavelengths, when they pass through a prism, a rainbow-like spectrum will be formed.)

When light is emitted by a small source, it travels off in all directions, and if nothing is in the way to absorb or reflect it, the emitted energy expands so that its leading edge forms the surface of an expanding sphere. If you think of the energy as photons, and the paths of those photons as rays, then if the source is far away, the rays passing through any small region will be essentially parallel. The rays heading for the array of prisms in figure 8.4 are all parallel. Therefore, they could have been emitted by a single light source far to the left, for example a star. All members of the group of rays passing through any one of the prisms are bent equally, but because the faces of the different prisms in figure 8.4 lie at different angles, the groups of rays converge. If you look care-

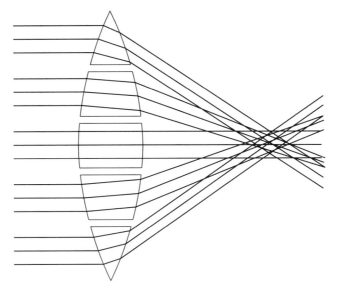

Figure 8.4. Groups of rays passing through a group of prisms with sides of differing slopes.

fully at the rays in figure 8.4, you will see that the angles of the prism faces have been chosen so that the rays at the center of each group converge to the same point, while the other rays in each group are parallel to their central ray.

The separate prism sections in figure 8.4 are each shaped so that, on the other side of the array of prisms, the central rays of each group converge to a single point. Obviously, if more and more thinner and thinner prism segments are stacked, and the angles of each are adjusted just right, the combination becomes a lens, as in figure 8.5, and all of the rays converge to the same point, the image of the distant source. That is, if the surfaces of the blob of glass are polished to just the right shape, it will form an image of the source. (Rays that miss the lens just keep going straight or might be absorbed by a lens mount. Those rays will be neglected in the rest of this discussion.) Note, here, that the diagram in figure 8.5 is only approximately correct. No lens can form a perfect image, for reasons that will be discussed later.

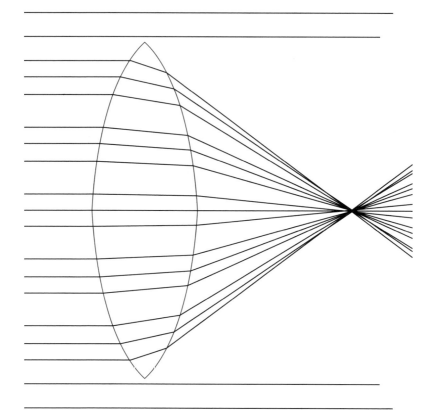

Figure 8.5. Same as figure 8.4, except that the thicknesses of the prisms have been made negligibly small. A lens!

Figure 8.6 (a) simply repeats what was shown in figure 8.5, a lens forming an image of a bright point, for example a distant star. (Of course there are many rays between the ones that are drawn. Those rays are omitted from the drawing for simplicity.) If the bright point is moved closer to the lens, rays arriving at the lens will be divergent but the lens will still form an image of the point, not quite as sharp an image, but an image, and the image will move farther from the lens (b). Similarly, if, somehow, the rays from the point are converging as they strike the lens, the same lens will form an image closer to itself (c).

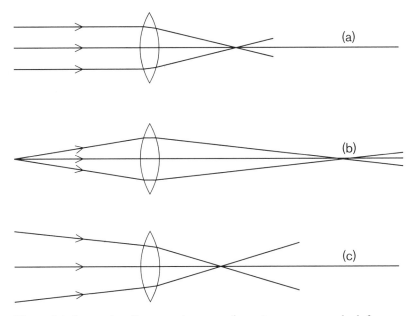

Figure 8.6. Lenses bending rays that come from tiny sources on the left at different distances. The rays in (a) are parallel, indicating that they come from a tiny source an infinite distance away. The rays in (b) come from a source near the lens, so they diverge. The angles these rays make when incident on the lens cause the rays to converge to an image (on the right) that is farther from the lens. The rays in (c) are converging. It is as though they came from a source farther away than infinity, but they could be converging because they passed through a lens before appearing in the drawing.

In some of these drawings, arrows are drawn indicating the direction of travel of photons, but in fact, if all the arrows were reversed, that is, if the photons were traveling in the opposite directions, the diagrams would still be correct. In general, in any optical system, a ray diagram indicates the paths of photons regardless of the directions they are traveling. If the image of a lightbulb is formed somewhere, putting the lightbulb where its image was will cause an image of the bulb to form where the bulb originally was. In optics, this is called the *principle of reciprocity*.

An interesting example of a phenomenon related to reciprocity is that sometimes, in a photograph of a face, the pupils appear red. Here's what's happening. If the source of the illumination is, for example, overhead lights, then the intensity of light entering the subject's eyes, reflecting from the retinas, coming back out of the eyes, and arriving at the camera is far less than the intensity reflected from the iris, the forehead, and other features in the scene, so the pupils look dark. But suppose the main source of illumination is small and right next to the lens of the camera, as is often the case with cellphone cameras. Some of the light from the phone's flash enters the subject's eyes, and the corneas and lenses in those eyes form images on the retinas, including a very bright spot corresponding to the flash. Then, by reciprocity, light reflected from the retina and exiting the pupil is acted on by the lens and cornea to form an image of the flash right back on top of the flash. That by itself will not produce red pupils, because that light won't enter the camera— the flash is close to the camera lens, but not in exactly the same place. However, when the light from the flash falls on the retina, some of it is scattered in the retinal tissue, and it also bounces around in the eyeball, so that the image of the flash is surrounded by scattered light, and the pattern imaged back on the camera is spread out. Therefore, if the flash is close to the camera lens, some of the light reflected from the retina enters the camera lens, lighting up the area of the image of the pupil. That light is predominantly red because the retinal tissues contain a lot of blood, which reflects red light most strongly.

This phenomenon can also be described in a different but closely related way. When taking a photograph with a source of light close to the lens of the camera, light from the source that is reflected from, say, the forehead scatters in all directions, so only a very small portion of it will enter the camera lens. However, light reflected from the image of the source on the retina and that spreads into neighboring tissue in the retina will be refracted by the lens and cornea of the eye so that instead of spreading widely, those rays will be concentrated at the camera.

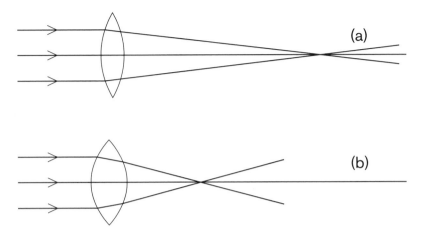

Figure 8.7. If the curvatures of the surfaces of a lens increase, they will bend the rays more strongly, so the image will be closer to the lens.

The sketch in figure 8.7 illustrates that if the curvature of the lens is made steeper, the angles at which the rays strike the glass and exit it increase, causing the image to move closer to the lens.

A very important point is illustrated in figure 8.8. Three separate point sources lie on the left side of the lens, at roughly equal distances from the lens. The lens will form an image of each of the sources. The relative positions of the images will be simply related to the relative positions of the sources, and each image will be formed independently of the others. To describe the sketch in figure 8.8 in a different way, on the left is an object that consists of three point sources, and on the right is an image of the object. *The image of the object, and the image of any object formed by a lens, is simply the sum of the images of each of the points on the object.*

Every scene can be considered as an array of points. Some of the points might be actual sources of light, but most of them are elements of the surfaces of things, for instance leaves or faces, that reflect a portion of the light incident on them. If the points in figure 8.8 were very close together and their images were slightly blurred, that is, slightly

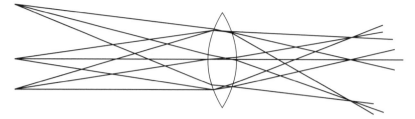

Figure 8.8. If a lens is not too thick, a ray going through its center will be essentially a straight line from the source to its image. Further, if different sources are about the same distance from a lens, the image of each of those sources will be about equally distant from the lens. The image of a point is the place where all the rays from that point converge. Therefore it is approximately true that the image of any point in a scene will be located on the straight line between the point and the center of the lens. Then if a scene is considered as a set of neighboring points, the image of the scene will simply be the sum of the rays that form the images of all the points in the scene.

out of focus, then their images, small spots of light, would overlap. Receptors lying under the overlapping regions would not distinguish between photons coming from the different spots and would simply absorb numbers of photons corresponding to the sums of the photons in the spots. The image of any scene is really the sum of the images of all of its points. With respect to vision, as you will see, this way of considering an image is especially useful in understanding processes related to images that are not sharply focused on the retina.

A lens can be shaped so that the rays from a point source on its axis will be bent just enough to converge to a small point. Although the surfaces of the lens might produce a sharp image of a point on its axis, images of points off to the side, "off-axis," will be somewhat blurred. This blurring can be reduced by shaping the lens as in figure 8.9. This is called a bent lens. So long as the thickness and angles are correct, it will form basically the same kinds of images as an unbent lens except that the images of off-axis points, like the upper and lower point sources in figure 8.9 and the central point source, hit the glass at exactly the correct angles to bring all the rays from that source to a fairly sharp point,

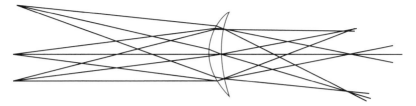

Figure 8.9. A bent lens. It will form an image in the same way as lenses that are not bent, but images of points not on the central axis will be sharper than they would be with an unbent lens.

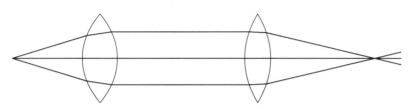

Figure 8.10. The photons approaching the lens on the right carry no information about where they came from. Therefore, a combination of lenses can be analyzed by considering only the angles between the surface of the lens and the rays that arrive at its surface.

and the bending of the lens allows an improvement in the sharpness of all off-axis points. That's why most spectacle lenses are bent.

Figure 8.10 illustrates another important point. Rays of light have no memory. For example, the lens on the left bends the rays from a nearby point source, and when the rays strike the second lens, they are exactly the same as they would have been if the source was far away and the first lens was not there; so the image, too, is the same as it would have been if the source was far away and the first lens was absent. The way a photon or a light wave behaves at any instant depends only on the medium it is traveling through and the direction it was traveling just before.

Note that each source of light in all of the figures above is a bright point. If the scene occupies more than one point, as in figures 8.8 and

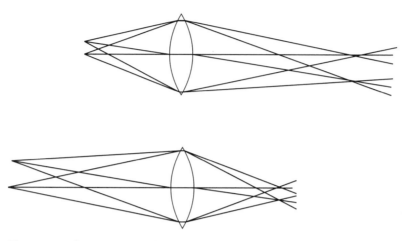

Figure 8.11. If a scene moves farther from a lens, the image of the scene will move closer to the lens and will have less magnification.

8.9, but the distance between the scene and the lens changes, then the image of each point in the scene remains almost a point but the distance between the images of the different points, that is, the *magnification* of the overall image, will vary with the distance. This is illustrated in figure 8.11.

Figure 8.12 illustrates the distribution of light at different distances from a lens forming an image of a point source. If a surface is moved from the lens toward the image, the pattern of light falling on the surface will have the same shape as the lens, in this example a circular disk, and as the surface moves farther from the lens, the disk becomes smaller, until, at the "image," the disk is as small as it can get. Then, if the surface is moved still farther away from the lens, the disk grows again. These disks are called blur circles. (If the lens were square, they should be "blur squares," but they are still called blur circles.)

Figure 8.13 illustrates what happens when a camera is pointed down toward a scene that stretches from close to the camera to fairly far from it. A lot of important aspects of imaging are illustrated here. First, the blur circles from the Christmas tree lights are obvious. (They are

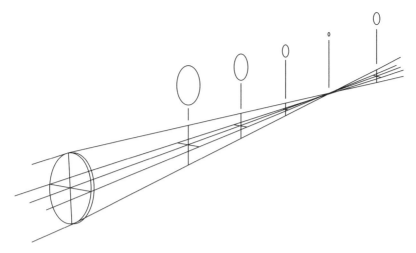

Figure 8.12. The distribution of light at different distances from a lens forming an image of a point source.

slightly elliptical because the camera, and therefore the lens in the camera that took the picture, was tilted somewhat downward.) The camera was focused near the middle distance in the image; the blur circles become smaller as they approach that distance and then grow larger beyond the focus, just as they were sketched in figure 8.12.

Below the center of the image, the blur circles from two bulbs overlap. The light intensity in the region where they overlap is actually the sum of the two intensities, but unfortunately the intensity of the each of the blur circles was greater than the maximum of the range of intensities that the camera could capture, and therefore the overlapping region appears at maximum brightness, just like each individual blur circle. However, you can see the blurring effect that overlapping blur circles have on an image by looking at the painting beneath the lights. Close to the lens, the blur circle from each point in the painting is large, so the blur circles from neighboring points in the painting overlap strongly. As the distance from the lens increases, the blur circles from the lights and from the points that make up the painting get smaller, so the images of neighboring points overlap less and the image is sharper. At still greater

Figure 8.13. This photograph illustrates several important points. First, the blur circles sketched in figure 8.11 are evident. Second, if two points of light are close together, their blur circles overlap. Third, the bigger the blur circles, the blurrier an image looks, because the blur circle from each point overlaps a larger region of its neighbors.

distances, the blur circles enlarge again and therefore the blurring increases.

The preceding way of describing optical phenomena, using "rays," involves thinking of light as streams of photons. Considering the wave-like properties of light leads to a different and more accurate way of understanding image formation. Reconsider any of the sketches in the preceding figures, but think of the light emerging from a single point in the object as a wave expanding from that point. Different parts of the wave will travel from the point to different places on the lens, through different parts of the lens, and then along different paths to the image. Along these paths, the wave will move through some particular number of cycles or fractions of a cycle on its way from the point to the lens, some additional number of cycles while in the lens, and then still more cycles when traveling between the lens and the image. When the ray is in the glass, the light will travel more slowly, and therefore the number of cycles per millimeter will be greater than when the ray passes through air.

Because the path lengths are different for paths through different parts of the lens, the number of cycles and fractions of a cycle will differ for each of those paths. It happens that there is only one location, on the image side of the lens, at which all of the light from a given point source travels along paths such that it oscillates through exactly the same number of cycles. Therefore there is only one place where all of the parts of the wave will be in phase, that is, only one place where all of the pieces of the wave go up and down exactly together. In that one location, all of the parts of the wave will add together to form a bright spot—everywhere else, some of the waves will be going up while others are going down, adding up to zero—and that one location is the image of the corresponding point on the object.

But that statement is slightly misleading. True, there is only one point where the pieces of the wave will be exactly in phase, but just slightly to the side of that point in any direction, they will be *almost* exactly in phase, so a spot very close to but not quite at the center of the image will be brighter than the background but not quite as bright as the center. Therefore the image of each point in a scene will not be a perfect point but will have its maximum brightness at the center, and the brightness will gradually trail off over a short distance around the center. That is what would be expected from a consideration of the wave-like properties of light, and it is precisely what actually happens. No matter how accurately a lens or system of lenses is constructed, an image is never a perfect replica of an object, but is always a little bit blurred due to the wave-like properties of light.

THE DEFINITION OF "IMAGE"

The slight blurring that results from the wave-like nature of light and the usually more significant blurring that results from defocusing (as in figure 8.13) illustrate a problem regarding the definition of the word "image." Images are always a little fuzzy, and so is the definition of the word "fuzzy." Reconsider figures 8.12 and 8.13, illustrating how the blur circle of the image of a point is related to the distance from the image of the point. If a screen were smoothly moved toward the lens from the plane where the image is most sharply focused, the blur circle from each point in the image would grow and the image would appear more and more blurred, until, when the screen lies up against the lens, the blur circles of all the points would equal the size of the lens and they would completely overlap. The "image" could then be described as totally defocused. But from the way the word "image" is used among people working with optics, it is not at all clear where, in this gradual motion of the screen and the corresponding change in blurring, the distribution of light falling on the screen should no longer be called an image. Certainly when the screen lies against the lens, the light on the screen is not called an image, but as soon as the screen begins to move away from the lens, some information about the features in the scene begins to appear in the light distribution. Where in that sequence the light distribution begins to be properly called an "image" is not clear.

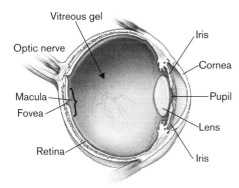

Figure 8.14. The human eye.

RETINAL IMAGE FORMATION

Here is figure 2.1 again, now called figure 8.14. Light from each of the points in the scene spreads in all directions, and some of it strikes the cornea. The front surface of the cornea acts in exactly the same way as one surface of a glass lens, except that glass slows down light a little more than the tissue of the cornea, so the rays are bent slightly less than they would be if they entered a glass lens of the same curvature. (The cornea also reflects a little of the incident light, about 2 percent, which is often called *glint.*)

The photons pass from the cornea into the aqueous humor, in which they travel at almost the same speed as in the tissue of the cornea, so the back surface of the cornea has almost no effect. Some of those photons then pass through the pupil and are incident on the crystalline lens. That lens is actually a very complicated onion-like structure, but, over-all, it acts like another simple lens, bending the rays more. The combined result of refraction at the cornea and through the crystalline lens produces an image of each point in the scene as a corresponding point on the retina—that is, a retinal image of the scene is created. Roughly two-thirds of the refractive power of the eye, the bending of rays that produces the retinal image, is provided by the surface between the air and the cornea. The remaining third is provided by the crystalline lens.

The preceding statements are only approximately true. Imperfections in the shapes of the cornea and lens spread the image of each point in the scene over a small but not infinitesimal region of the retina, causing the light from neighboring regions to overlap and the retinal image to be somewhat blurred. Further, remember that the greater the distance from a point in the scene to the eye, the shorter is the distance from the cornea to the plane where the image is sharply focused (as illustrated in figure 8.6), so points in the scene that are at different distances from the eye cannot all be in sharp focus on the retina at the same time. And when the curvatures of your cornea and lens form images in planes that are not in the plane of the photoreceptors, the retinal image will be blurred. That is what eye care professionals are for, as explained in the next chapter.

But if you have good vision, when you look at a typical outdoor scene everything in the distance seems to be in sharp focus, regardless of how far away it is. That seems to contradict some of the preceding discussion. The reasons that it is not contradictory are explained in chapter 9.

EYE MOVEMENTS

Eyes can move in a lot of different ways. They can translate (that is, shift without rotating) sideways or up and down when your head moves, and they can translate a little even when your head doesn't move, because the eyeball sits in a chamber lined with muscle and fat. They can also rotate about a vertical axis, to look to the side, or about a horizontal axis, to look up or down. If you tilt your head to the side your eyes start to get rotated about another horizontal axis, the line of sight, thus rotating the retina with respect to the retinal image, but another set of muscles attached to the eyes drives them to rotate in the opposite direction, canceling the rotation of the retinal image with respect to the retina.

The term "eye movement" almost always refers only to rotational movements, not translational ones. Translations are very rarely interesting because they usually have negligible effects on vision. For example, suppose you look from the left edge of the moon to the right edge. The moon subtends almost exactly one-half of a degree of "visual angle," so to look from the left edge of the moon to the right edge, you rotate your eyes through half a degree. When you do that, the front of your eye moves to the right through about 0.1 millimeter (and the back of your eye moves about the same distance in the opposite direction). If, instead, you look at the left edge of the moon and then *translate* your head or eye sideways 0.1 mm without any rotation, you won't be looking at the right edge of the moon, you will be looking at a point on the moon that is 0.1 mm from its left edge.

Most cellphones include a camera, which consists of a tiny lens and a very small electronic image sensor. The sensor and its associated circuitry convert the image into electronic form and display an enlarged version of it on a screen. If you have a cellphone or a camera, try this. Point the camera so that the image of some object is roughly centered on the screen. Shift the camera sideways a little without rotating it, and the display will hardly change. Both the image and the whole camera have moved together. Then swivel, that is rotate, the camera a little. The image of the object will seem to move a lot. Although it appears that the image moved, what really happened was that the image stayed essentially in the same place in the world but the sensor shifted sideways under the image. The same thing happens when you rotate your eyes. The retina slides under the image.

There is a tiny region near the center of the retina, called the fovea, where the receptors are packed very tightly together. If you decide to look at something, say a particular star (just to simplify this discussion, assume that one eye is covered), what your visual system does is to activate muscles attached to the eyeball, causing it to rotate so that the image of the star falls on the fovea. What actually happens is that the retinal image of the star remains essentially in the same place but the retina slides underneath it in such a way that the fovea now sits under the image of the star.

Now suppose you decide to look instead at the moon. Before your eye starts to move to look at the moon, the retinal image of the moon will lie at some distance from the fovea. Your visual system will make a series of computations and then cause your eyeball to rotate extremely quickly, and when the movement stops, the image of the moon is centered on the fovea. (Those computations and the nature of the ensuing movement are very interesting but beyond the scope of the discussion here.)

THINGS TO THINK ABOUT

1. Surprisingly often, in night scenes on television and in movies, there are colored disks in the background, which you may not have noticed but maybe will notice from now on. Occasionally, they are not disks but rather uniformly bright and colored spots with hexagonal or octagonal edges. Why?
2. Sometimes something, for example fine print, is hard to see clearly and it helps to shine more light on it, even when the original lighting is intense enough that the rods are not involved. Why does more light help?

RELEVANT READING

Comprehensive coverage of research on eye movements:
Simon P. Liversedge, Iain D. Gilchrist, and Stefan Everling (eds.). 2011. *Oxford Handbook of Eye Movements*. Oxford: Oxford University Press.

CHAPTER NINE

Optometrists, Ophthalmologists, Opticians: What They Do

There is often confusion about the work done by opticians, optometrists, and ophthalmologists. Now that the optics required to understand some of their procedures has been covered, here's a brief description of what each of them does. Then each description will be given in more detail and the science that supports and explains why they do what they do will be discussed. (The qualifications for each of these professions and the specifics of what they actually do differ significantly from country to country; this discussion will be confined to their roles in the United States.)

Ophthalmologists examine eyes looking for pathologies, using drugs or surgery to treat any they find, and they evaluate visual acuity, finding and writing prescriptions for glasses if they are needed. Ophthalmologists have graduated from medical school with an MD (doctor of medicine) or a DO (doctor of osteopathy) degree, and typically have had three or four years of advanced training in ophthalmology.

Optometrists also examine eyes looking for pathologies, and evaluate visual acuity, finding and writing prescriptions for glasses if they are needed. Optometrists treat some pathologies with drugs and surgery, but the range of drugs they are permitted to prescribe and the range of surgeries they are licensed to perform is much more restricted than the range for ophthalmologists, and that range varies widely from state to state within the United States. Optometrists usually have completed an undergraduate college degree and three to five years of postgraduate training at a school of optometry, for which they are awarded a degree called an OD, for doctor of optometry (OD, not DO).

Opticians fit eyeglasses and contact lenses according to the prescriptions written by optometrists and ophthalmologists. In some countries other than the United States, opticians also perform eye examinations. (In the Unites States and elsewhere, people who build optical instruments such as telescopes are also called opticians.)

One of the main things that both optometrists and ophthalmologists do is to find a prescription for glasses or contact lenses that correct defects in the optics of an eye, the process they call *refraction*. To do that, many ophthalmologists and optometrists use a device called an autorefractor. You look into the device for a few seconds and it then prints out a prescription that is close to what you need for glasses. Some ophthalmologists use that result directly as a prescription, but many ophthalmologists and almost all optometrists use the result as a starting place for a manual refraction, which proceeds like this.

You sit in a chair and look through a device called a phoropter, which allows the examiner to put any of a large variety of lenses in front of your eye. You see a chart that usually contains rows of letters of decreasing size. The path from the eye to the chart should be at least 20 feet long (which is often arranged, if the room isn't long enough, by reflecting the chart from a mirror). If your vision is "normal" and no lens (or a lens of zero power) is between you and the chart, you will be able to correctly read the letters in a particular line near the bottom of the chart. If you had been tested by an autorefractor, the doctor or ophthalmic assistant may have entered the autorefractor result into the phoropter, which positions the appropriate lens in front of your eye, and you will probably be able to read that line or at least some of its letters. Then the examiner will use the phoropter to try other lenses, in a systematic and somewhat complicated procedure, to find the lens that allows you to read the smallest line of letters that you can.

The cornea has a certain curvature, and there is a lens inside your eye, right behind the iris. The combination of those surfaces acts like a single lens, forming an image of the test chart on or near your retina, as explained in chapter 8. If you have "normal" vision, then without glasses or the lenses in the phoropter, that combination of curvatures will bend the rays just strongly enough to form a sharp image right in the plane of your retina. But suppose your eyeball is a little bit shorter, so that the image of the chart would be heading to be sharp behind your retina. Then the image that actually falls on the photoreceptors in your retina will be out of focus, light from each point on the chart will spread in a blur circle to overlap with light from neighboring points, and your visual acuity will be reduced. (If you are less than about forty years old, the lens inside your eye will increase its curvature, bringing the image into sharp focus, but a discussion of that complication will be held off until later.) This condition, in which the image of the scene would be sharply focused in a plane behind the retina, is called hypermetropia, or sometimes, misleadingly, "farsightedness." It affects about one-quarter of the population in the United States.

Figure 9.1 is a sketch representing hypermetropia. This and the following sketches are simplified in that they omit the crystalline lens, the thickness of the cornea, and so on, and it is assumed that the scene, for instance an eye chart, is at least 20 feet away, so that the rays from each single point on the chart are essentially parallel. (Rays from a different point on the chart will also be parallel to each other, but will lie at an angle to the rays from the first point.) The rays from each point on the chart are bent by the optics of the eye so that they would focus behind the retina, and therefore they form overlapping blur circles on the retina. The rays are not converging strongly enough.

Now suppose the examiner positions a lens in the phoropter that causes the rays from each point on the chart to converge a little before they get to your eye, as in figure 9.2. Then the rays heading for your retina will converge a little more than they did without the phoropter lens. If the power of the lens in the phoropter is just right, it will cause

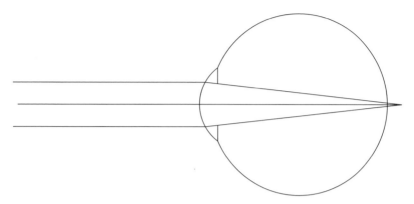

Figure 9.1. An eye in which the cornea and lens do not provide strong enough refraction to cause rays from a distant point to converge at the retina. A blur circle is produced on the retina.

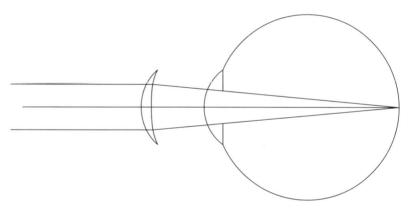

Figure 9.2. A spectacle lens in front of the eye in figure 9.1 causes the rays to converge a little before they arrive at the eye, so that the rays converge at the retina.

the rays to focus right at your retina, the blur circles will be very small, and you will be able to see smaller, finer letters. In general, the eye doctor moves a lens into and out of the path between your eye and the chart and asks you which looks sharper, and in that way searches for the lens that will give you the best vision.

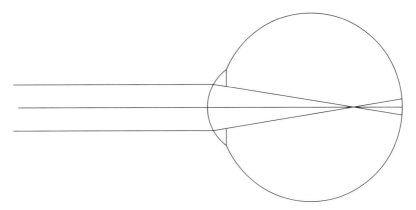

Figure 9.3. The refractive power of this eye causes the rays from a distant point to converge to form a sharp image of the point before they reach the retina, producing a blur circle on the retina. This eye is "nearsighted."

Figure 9.3 illustrates what happens if your eyeball is too long. This is called myopia, or "nearsightedness." The image is formed sharply in front of the retina, so, again, the image of the chart that falls on the retina is blurred. This can be corrected by positioning a lens in the phoropter that causes the rays to *diverge* a little before they enter the eye (figure 9.4). Such a lens, instead of bulging in the middle, is thinner in the middle than at the edges, and is called a "negative" lens.

Why is this condition called nearsightedness? During the procedure described so far, the eye chart is about 20 feet away from the eye. If you have "normal" vision or are looking through a lens that corrects your vision for distant objects, the retinal image will be in sharp focus on the retina for all objects 20 feet or more away. That is, moving from 20 to, say, 1,000 feet will produce a negligible change in the distance from the cornea to the plane where the image is sharpest. If, instead, your retina lies beyond where the image of a distant scene is sharply focused (your eyeball is too long), the image of a distant scene will be blurred. But, as was illustrated in figure 8.5 (p. XXX), when the scene gets closer to the eye, the in-focus plane of the image moves away from the lens. If you are nearsighted, when the scene gets near enough, the image will be in

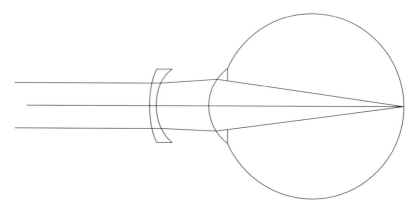

Figure 9.4. A spectacle lens that is thinner at the center than at the edges causes the rays to diverge a little before they reach the eye, so the image of a distant point is formed sharply on the retina. The "negative" lens thus corrects nearsightedness.

focus on your retina. Distant things will be blurry but nearer things will be sharp, so you are "nearsighted."

ACCOMMODATION

The lens inside the eye, the crystalline lens, is held in place by a thin transparent capsule, and the capsule is surrounded by a muscle and a complicated attachment such that when the muscle contracts, and if the lens is flexible enough, the lens will bulge more. That is, the curvature of the surfaces of the lens, mostly its front surface, can increase so it bends the incoming rays more strongly and the image of the scene moves toward the front of the eye. That process is called *accommodation*.

If you have "normal" vision, that is, if your eyes are like the average person's, then when you look at something far away, the curvatures of your cornea and lens combine so that the image of the distant scene is in focus on your retinas. Then, suppose you want to look at something close, for instance read a book. Because when you first look at the book, it is closer that what you were focused on before, the plane of focus of the retinal image of the book will lie behind the retina and be out of focus on the retina. Then the muscles controlling the lens in your eyes will cause the lens to bulge more, moving the image forward until it is in focus on the retina. You have accommodated.

As you get older, the lens becomes less flexible and you are less and less able to accommodate. By the time you are about forty, the lens has become too stiff to appreciably change its curvature, so when you try to read, you can't focus the image of the print on your retinas; you need reading glasses. Reading glasses just contain lenses that cause the rays to converge a little before they enter your eyes. The closer you normally hold the book, the stronger the lenses you'll need for reading.

When you look at an eye chart through a phoropter, the chart is set to be about 20 feet away, and when you are correctly focused for something that far away, focus will be essentially just as good for anything farther away than that. But as things move closer and if the lenses in your eyes can't change their power enough, the change in focus will become noticeable. The condition when your lenses are not flexible enough to change their power is called presbyopia, and your eye doctor will add the appropriate information to your prescription. If your vision is otherwise normal, that is, if you are neither myopic nor hypermetropic, you may use a pair of reading glasses when you want to see near objects clearly. If you are myopic or hypermetropic, you may instead choose to wear *bifocals,* that is, lenses such that the upper sections provide a correction for distant vision and the lower segments have the right amount of added curvature to bring near objects into focus on your retinas.

If you have "normal" vision or if you are wearing glasses with the right prescription, the cornea and lens in your eye, together, form an image of an eye chart, or any other object 20 feet away, that is sharply focused in the plane of your retina. Then each point on all objects nearer than or farther than 20 feet from your eye will form blur circles, as was shown in figure 8.11 (p. XXX), and so should look blurred. Things a lot closer than 20 feet do look blurry—unless you can accommodate on them or are wearing bifocals or reading glasses—but things farther

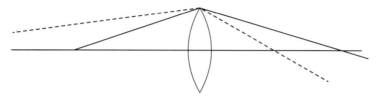

Figure 9.5. The image of a point will move away from a lens as the point approaches the lens.

away than that don't look blurry. In fact, if you look out the window, everything looks pretty sharp, even the moon. What's going on?

If the retinal images of things 20 feet away are sharply focused on your retina, it is true that things farther away will be a little out of focus, that is, each point on a more distant object will form a blur circle, but the blur circles of points beyond 20 feet or so will be so small that the blur they cause will not be noticeable.

Figure 9.5 shows one ray (the solid line) from a nearby source on the left that hits close to the edge of a lens, and another ray (the dashed line) from a source farther away that hits the same place on the lens. The distance between the lens and the image depends on the angle between the incoming ray and the axis of the lens, that is, the horizontal line. Now suppose the source moves farther from the lens in one-foot steps. As the distance between the lens and the source increases, the angle between the ray and the axis decreases (so the image moves closer to the lens), but as the source gets farther away from the lens, each one-foot step causes a smaller and smaller change in the angle between the ray and the axis, so, as the source gets farther away, the changes in its distance make less and less difference. For instance, when the source moves from 20 feet away to 100 feet away, the angle hardly changes at all, and so the image moves only a very tiny bit closer to the lens.

Figure 9.6 is a plot showing how the distance from the lens to the image changes in relation to the change in distance from the source to the lens. (The relationship is simply that the distance of the image in inversely proportional to the distance of the source.) The distance of

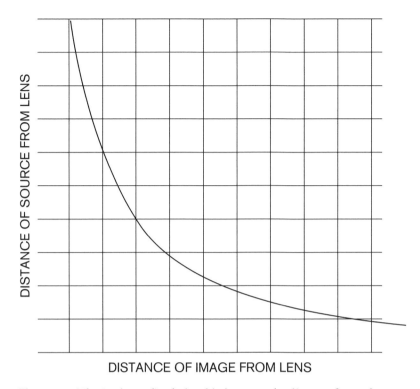

DISTANCE OF IMAGE FROM LENS

Figure 9.6. The (reciprocal) relationship between the distance from a lens to an object and the distance from the lens to the image of the object.

the image from the lens (or from the retina) changes much more slowly when the source is far away. Therefore, the size of the blur circles on the retina and thus the sharpness of the image on the retina also hardly changes when distant things get more distant.

Here are some specific numbers for human eyes. To examine fine detail, your eyes rotate so that the retinal image of the detail falls on a small region at the center of the retina, the fovea, that contains only cones. The human eyeball is about 25 millimeters in diameter, and the parts of the cones that contain visual pigment form a layer about 0.05 mm thick near the back surface of the retina. If the eye is correctly focused so that the retinal image of an object 20 feet away is sharply imaged on the layer of cones, and then the object is moved to reading distance, say 1 foot away (and the lens in the eye does not change its optical power), the plane at which the retinal image would be sharpest will move about 0.72 mm farther from the front of the eye. For an average-sized pupil, that would form blur circles about 0.16 mm in diameter. If instead the object moved from 20 feet to 10,000 feet away, the image would move only 0.05 mm forward, and the blur circles would be less than 0.01 mm in diameter. That's about the size of an ideal retinal image of a dot less than 2.5 mm wide and 20 feet away. So although blur circles are formed in an out-of-focus image no matter how far away the object is, the blur circles are very tiny and hardly differ at all for objects farther away than 20 feet or so.

There is one more step that the eye doctor will perform when determining your prescription for glasses, a step that is difficult to perform and also difficult to explain. The discussion so far works if the optics of the eye are like a simple lens, circularly symmetric. But think about the cornea. It is a thin transparent shell of flexible tissue, and it provides about two-thirds of the refracting power of the eye. Suppose you put a finger on the eyelid that's covering the top of your cornea, and your thumb on the lid covering the lower part of your cornea, and then squeeze a little. That will make the curvature of the cornea steeper in the vertical direction than it is in the horizontal direction, so rays hitting above and below the center of the cornea will converge more strongly than rays hitting to the left and right of the center. If you were looking at a star, the horizontally positioned rays might be in focus but then the vertical ones would converge in front of the retina and they would form a blurred vertical line where they hit the retina. If you were focused on the vertical rays, the retina image would be a blurred horizontal line.

Having a cornea with the curvature at one angle that is different from the curvature at the perpendicular angle is common. (Although the angles are often close to vertical or horizontal, they are not necessarily.) This condition is called astigmatism. To correct it, a lens is needed that is asymmetric in the opposite way. (An example of a highly astigmatic lens is a glass rod, a "cylindrical lens." Along its long axis, the curvature is zero.) Some of the lenses in the phoropter are cylindrical lenses of various powers. By turning knobs, the examiner can select a cylindrical lens of some power and add it into the viewing path, and also change the angle of the cylinder, to try to find the power and angle that best corrects any astigmatism in your eye. You can see how this is a tricky procedure, because both the power and the angle have to be right, so the examiner can't just pick a power and vary its angle until your acuity is best, both power and angle have to be varied together. Trying to find a golf ball in a two-dimensional field is a lot harder than finding it in a trough.

The final result of the refraction process is a list that would look something like this as an example:

OD	*OS*
Sphere 1.50	Sphere 1.25
Cylinder 1.00	Cylinder 1.00
Axis 78	Axis 82

OD stands for right eye, OS for left eye. The glasses are then made with one surface, for instance the side away from your eye, having the (circularly symmetric) curvature required to correct the focus error for a distant target, neglecting astigmatism. That curvature requirement is labeled Sphere. The cylindrical power, Cylinder, is ground or molded into the other surface of the glass. When each lens is mounted in glasses frames, the angle of the cylindrical component is positioned according to the angle called Axis, zero degrees being horizontal, 30 degrees being tilted so that the axis rises from left to right, and so on. (If your astigmatism is too small to bother correcting, the power of the cylinder required will be zero and in the prescription may be labeled *plano*.)

From that description, you might expect that the lenses in a pair of glasses would look basically flat, with a little spherical curvature on one side and a little cylindrical curvature on the other. If the glasses were actually made that way, they would work well so long as you were looking straight ahead, but if you looked toward the side, your retinal images would be somewhat distorted. To reduce that distortion, more, equal, curvature is added to both sides of each lens, that is, the lens is "bent" (as in figure 8.8, p. 84), so that both surfaces of the lens bulge forward.

If you are presbyopic, that is, if the lenses in your eyes aren't flexible enough for you to accommodate, and if you decide you want bifocals, the examiner might add a parameter called *add* to your prescription. Then when the lenses are made, part of the outside surface of the lower region of the lenses will be given more curvature so that when you look through that region, closer things will be in focus. (There are also more complicated ways to provide near vision. For instance, lenses called *progressive* can be made so that the power of the lenses smoothly increases as you look through from the top to the bottom. That way, the lower your line of sight through the glasses, the greater is the extra power provided for near vision. Alternatively, if you wear contact lenses, the power of the lens for one eye can be correct for distance vision and the lens for the other eye can have a power appropriate for near vision. Or, the power at the center of a contact lens can be made to be correct for distance vision and the power in a ring around that central region can be correct for near vision. Those techniques add together a somewhat defocused retinal image and a sharp one, and for many people that works.)

Usually, an eye doctor will also use a device called a slit lamp to examine the front of your eyes. A slit lamp is really nothing but a head and chin rest for you, a source of light that can be shaped into a slit, and a binocular microscope that provides the doctor a magnified three-dimensional view. For some purposes, the doctor uses the slit lamp just to provide a magnified and well-lighted look at your cornea, lids, and iris. For other purposes, the examiner might apply anesthetic drops to the front of your eye and touch the cornea with an instrument that measures the pressure inside the eye. Ophthalmologists and optometrists routinely perform these and many other tests to screen for or evaluate medical conditions such as glaucoma and cataracts. The medical aspects of these tests will not be discussed, but here are a few common, simple conditions that are frequently asked about.

CATARACTS

The molecules that make up the eye lens and the cornea are arranged in an orderly matrix, and the orderliness of that matrix enables the lens and corneal tissue to be transparent. Any disturbance of the orderliness spoils the transparency and causes light to scatter away from the paths it would otherwise take. The things called cataracts are regions of the eye lens that, usually as a consequence of the accumulation of tiny injuries through the years, have lost their orderliness and so scatter light. Cataracts do absorb a small portion of the light passing through them, but that absorption has a negligible effect on vision. (After all, sunglasses absorb light too.) It is the scattering of light that causes essentially all of the harmful effects of cataracts.

Almost everyone over the age of forty or so begins to develop small cataractous spots in their lenses, spots which at first have virtually no effect on vision, but with age, those spots do slowly accumulate and get larger until they have noticeable effects. They reduce visual acuity somewhat because the scattered light reduces the contrast in the retinal image, but people usually become bothered by the scattering only when the glare from bright lights, especially automobile headlights, makes seeing noticeably difficult. Devices exist that provide measures of the effects of glare on vision, but most eye doctors decide whether or not to advise a corrective procedure either by using a slit lamp to observe the haziness, the amount of scattering, directly, or by relying on the patient's judgement of impairment. (Acuity, as measured by an eye chart, is not a reliable measure of the need for cataract surgery.)

The corrective procedure that is almost always used involves removing the entire cataractous lens and replacing it with a plastic one. The procedure is quick and relatively painless, and complications are rare. Some time before the procedure, the patient looks into an instrument or set of instruments that measure the length of the eyeball, the curvature of the cornea, and sometimes a few other dimensions, providing the information needed to select the appropriate plastic lens. Then, under local anesthesia (usually preceded by a mild sedative), the surgeon makes a small incision near the outer edge of the cornea and inserts a hollow needle into the lens. The needle delivers an ultrasonic vibration that liquefies the tissue of the lens, and the liquid is drawn out. Then the surgeon inserts a small plastic lens, known as an IOL (intraocular lens), and closes the incision with a stitch if needed. The patient wears a patch to cover that eye, and goes home. Recovery is usually complete in about a week. (Cataracts typically develop at roughly the same rate in both eyes, but when corrective surgery is performed, it is almost always done on only one eye, with a waiting period of at least a month before operating on the other eye.)

FLOATERS

The inside of the eyeball is filled with a jelly-like substance called the vitreous humor, as in figures 2.1 (p. xxx) and 8.13 (p. xxx). What doesn't show in those figures is a very thin layer of fluid that lies between the vitreous humor and the surface of the retina. That fluid often contains what amounts to eyeball trash: stray blood corpuscles, remnants of pigment shed from the retina, and fibers from the vitreous humor. Those particles cast shadows on the retina. If they were tightly attached to the retina, like the blood vessels are, we would not see them, as discussed in chapter 5. But they are floating in that thin layer of fluid between the vitreous humor and the retina. When the eyeball moves, the vitreous sloshes around and the fluid, along with its trash, gets squeezed and moves relative to the retina.

Seeing floaters is usually not a sign of pathology. We normally have a few and acquire more and more as we age. However, an abrupt jump in the number of floaters can indicate a problem, so if you suddenly start seeing a lot of floaters, it is a good idea to visit an eye doctor. The vitreous humor sometimes makes attachments to the retina. With age, the vitreous humor shrinks, and in older people it can suddenly pull away from the retina, causing the release of a shower of floaters. Usually (in about 85 percent of cases) that is a harmless event (except for the annoyance of seeing more floaters), but sometimes the *retina* also pulls away from the back of the eye, and that can be serious, so it is important to see an eye doctor right away if you see a sudden shower of floaters.

MIGRAINE AURAS

Some people experience a visual phenomenon called an aura, usually preceding a migraine headache. A first encounter with a migraine visual aura can be frightening. The series of events differs from time to time and among different people, but in general the first symptom is a blind spot, often right in the center of vision, about the size of a letter of print, and binocular—that is, it looks the same no matter which eye the person is looking out of. Usually the blind spot enlarges and spreads in a flickering zig-zag spiral and lasts for several minutes.

The cause of such auras is unknown (as is the cause of migraines), but, since they look the same using either eye, they are clearly a result of some event in the brain, not in the eyeball. Although auras are frightening and often result in a visit to an eye doctor, they rarely indicate pathology, and are simply disturbing when they are going on.

COLORS THAT DIFFER BETWEEN EYES

Occasionally you may notice that the colors in the scene look somewhat different depending upon which eye you are seeing with. There are two common causes of this condition. If the color difference is always pretty much the same, that is, for instance, if things always look a little yellower when looking out of your right eye, the color difference is probably the result of a difference in the coloration of the crystalline lenses in the two eyes. As we age, crystalline lenses become yellower, and a difference in the rate of this process between the two eyes can cause apparent color differences in the scene. So long as this difference is not severe, it is the result of normal aging.

A more common cause of interocular color differences is the following. In chapter 3, light and dark adaptation were discussed, and color vision will be discussed in chapter 10. Both are relevant here. Almost always, when we are seeing, depending on the angle of our heads relative to the scene, the light incident on one eye is slightly different in average or overall color and intensity from the light falling on the other eye. If, say, the light forming the retinal image in the right eye contains, on average, more long-wavelength, red energy than in the left, then because of adaptation, sensitivity to reddish colors will be reduced in the right eye relative to the left, so things will look redder when looking out of the left eye. So long as such a difference in color or brightness is mild, it does not indicate pathology.

THINGS TO THINK ABOUT

Sometimes an eye doctor will put drops in the patient's eyes. The chemical in one kind of drop anesthetizes the cornea so the doctor can touch the cornea without producing pain. (The cornea is often touched in a test for glaucoma.) Another chemical causes the pupil to dilate. A third kind of chemical essentially paralyzes the muscle that causes the lens in the eye to change its shape.

1. Why would it be useful to dilate your pupils?
2. Why would it be useful to paralyze the lens muscle? (Hint: it would only be useful if you are less than about 40 years old).
3. It has often been suggested that the reason some artists draw or paint scenes that are very distorted—think of Salvador Dali—is because they have very distorted vision. Explain why that makes sense or is nonsense.
4. Suppose you look at a colon (: that one) through a magnifying glass. Explain, using a diagram of the rays, why the colon appears magnified.

CHAPTER TEN

Color Vision

Color vision is a huge topic. Many books and thousands of research papers have been written about it. You have already read, in chapters 2, 3, and 8, about the major visual processes that underlie seeing colors. Some of these processes lead to surprising phenomena. For instance, if you look at a red light, its usually looks red, but if the light is very bright, it will look red at first, then rapidly change through yellow to green, and then slowly back through yellow to orange. The reason for those changes will become clear from an understanding of the physiological bases of color vision.

The retinas of people with normal visual systems contain both kinds of photoreceptors, rods and cones. However, a few people have retinas that contain only rods, so while their visual sensitivity in very dim light is normal, everything looks equally glaringly bright at daylight levels.

Remember, as you read in chapter 1, that wavelength is the distance, as a wave travels, between each peak and the next peak, and the amount of energy that a wave delivers to a detector varies inversely with wavelength, so each photon with a short wavelength will deliver more energy to a detector than each photon with a longer wavelength. Figure 3.3, copied here as figure 10.1, is the absorption spectrum of the visual pigment in rods. (This curve and the ones that follow are not plotted at

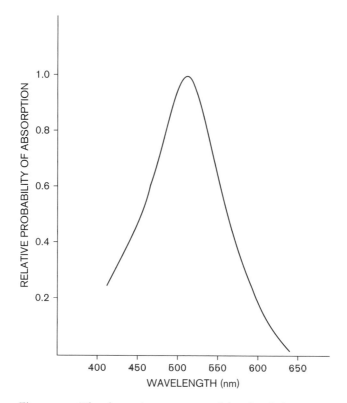

Figure 10.1. The absorption spectrum of the visual pigment in rods.

their short-wavelength ends because their measurement there is too difficult to perform reliably.)

In figure 10.1, the relative likelihood that a photon will be absorbed by a rod pigment molecule (and trigger an isomerization and visual response) is plotted as a function of the wavelength of the photon (nm stands for nanometer, a thousandth of a millionth of a meter). A crucial property of every rod, but something that is not obvious from the figure, is the following: if a photon is absorbed, the effect on the rest of the visual system is *exactly the same regardless of the wavelength of the absorbed photon.* The wavelength does affect the likelihood that a photon will be absorbed, but if a photon *is* absorbed, the molecule isomerizes and closes a hole in the membrane, as described in chapter 3, in precisely the same way regardless of the wavelength of the photon. (Each pigment molecule absorbs photons over a range of different wavelengths and energies, and differences in the energies of absorbed photons just cause slight differences in the temperature of the molecule.) Therefore, a person whose retinas contain only one kind of pigment is *wavelength-blind*. This condition is usually called total color blindness, but that is a slightly misleading label. What is missing is the ability to sense information about the wavelengths contained in the retinal image. If a light is presented to a person who has only rods and the wavelength of the light is varied, the person will see a light whose brightness varies. The person will not be able to tell the difference between changing the wavelength of the light and changing its intensity.

0

PHOTON ABSORPTIONS

Figure 10.2. A representation of the effect of light on a visual system that contains only rods, when the wavelength or intensity of the light, or both, is varied. The effect on the rods varies along only one dimension.

Because every absorbed photon has an identical effect on a pigment molecule regardless of its wavelength, if photons of several different wavelengths are absorbed, their effects simply add together and produce excitation that is exactly the same as increasing the number of incident photons of a single wavelength. So long as the wavelength is within the range of the absorption spectrum of rod pigment, increasing the rate of photons incident on a rod increases the strength of its excitation regardless of the wavelengths of the photons. The output of a rod can only vary along one dimension, as illustrated in figure 10.2.

As a result, rods can be said to be totally color-blind, or, more accurately, totally wavelength-blind. Different parts of any scene produce excitations that vary in only one dimension regardless of the wavelengths in the scene. The appearance of the scene will vary only in what we call brightness. To describe the situation a different way, suppose this person were shown two spots side by side, each illuminated by a different wavelength or intensity, or a different mixture of wavelengths and intensities. The two spots would probably look different. Each could be represented by a different point along the axis in figure 10.2. However, the two spots could be made to be plotted at the same point, that is, could be made to look identical, by adjusting only one thing, the intensity *or* the wavelength of one of the spots.

The light from the sun contains a broad range of wavelengths, and almost all objects reflect a broad range. (Very few objects reflect only a single wavelength.) A ripe banana strongly reflects a group of wavelengths centered around 575 nm, while an unripe one reflects a group more strongly centered around 550 nm. To a person (or his ancestor) with only rods, an unripe banana in sunlight would probably look brighter than a ripe banana, but if the unripe one were in shadow, it could well look the same as the ripe one, or even less bright. In other words, a person with only rods would not be able to distinguish ripe from unripe bananas. Just changing the illumination level could change their appearance from ripe to unripe.

In dim light, all of us are like a person without cones, because the cones, being much less sensitive than the rods, don't deliver signals at low light levels. But in the normal retina, there are both rods and cones, and three different kinds of cones are present, each containing a slightly different pigment. As explained in the following, when the light level is high enough, the cones provide outputs carrying information about both the intensities and the wavelengths in a scene.

The absorption spectra of the three different kinds of cones are plotted in figure 10.3. The naming of these three requires some discussion. Imagine seeing a light of a very long wavelength, for example 700 nm. At a low intensity, it will look dark. As the intensity is increased, it will begin to excite the cones that have the absorption spectrum that is farthest to the right in figure 10.3 but will not be intense enough to cause a noticeable excitation in any of the other kinds of cones, and it will look red. (As the intensity continues to increase, it will appear brighter, but

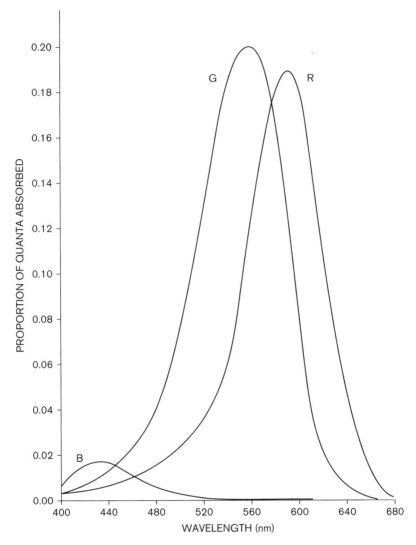

Figure 10.3. The absorption spectra of the three kinds of visual pigment in the cones of most human retinas.

it would boil the retina before it became intense enough to begin significantly exciting any of the other kinds of cones.) Similarly, a short
wavelength, for example 410 nm, will most strongly excite the cones
with the absorption spectrum farthest to the left, and will appear blue.
But it will also excite the R and G cones and so will not appear "pure"
blue; it will appear as if whiteness has been added to it, as explained
below. Light of wavelengths in the middle looks green.

Therefore, for a long time, the three kinds of cones were labeled for
the hues they generated, R (red), G (green), and B (blue), as in figure 10.3.
However, people doing basic research on the mechanisms of color vision
believe that it is important to distinguish between the appearance of a
spot of light and its underlying physics and physiology, and they began,
instead, to refer to the three kinds of cones with reference to the wavelengths at the highest points in their absorption spectra, as L (long), M
(medium), and S (short). In the early drafts of this book, they were
referred to as L, M, and S, but in working on the drafts, it was clear that
the reader, in his or her head, continually had to translate from the L, M,
S labels into the R, G, and B labels in order to follow the logic, so it was
decided to use the R, G, and B labels in these discussions.

The naming of the visual pigment is actually interesting and inform-
ative. For example, consider the pigment labeled B. It is usually called
the "blue" pigment, but the pigment itself isn't blue. If you looked at a
pile of B pigment illuminated by ordinary white light, it wouldn't look
blue. In fact, it would have a hue that could be called the *opposite* of blue:
it would look yellow. Here's why. "Ordinary" light, which we call white,
is a mixture of wavelengths and intensities such that all three kinds of
cones absorb photons at roughly equal rates. A pile of B pigment will
most strongly absorb the short-wavelength photons in the incident light
and so will reflect, about equally, a mixture of photons that have medium
and long wavelengths. That mixture produces an excitation pattern that
we call yellow. (Looking at figure 10.3, you can see that light of a single
wavelength, around 575 nm, will also be absorbed by the R and the G
cones equally, and we call that yellow.)

So, to seem more correct, we could say that the B pigment is the one that absorbs *blue photons* most strongly. That, too, would be misleading. Short-wavelength photons are not blue. They're just waves or particles of energy. The hue comes from our neurology, after photons are absorbed.

That's why people who study color vision label the pigments S, M, and L. Nevertheless, for ease in keeping track of the explanations here, they will be labeled B, G, and R, with apologies to color experts.

The plot in figure 10.3 shows that the B pigment absorbs maximally at about 430 nm, the G pigment at about 550 nm, and the R at 620 nm. The absorption curves for people with normal color vision can vary somewhat both in height and in position along the wavelength axis, so consider these curves as only representative of a typical visual system.

Note that the curves in figure 10.3 are *absorption* spectra, that is, they plot the proportion of incident photons that are absorbed by each class of cones. At light levels low enough to be close to the thresholds for these cones, the curves also properly represent the *excitation* of each cone system as a function of wavelength, because at low light levels, excitation is probably directly proportional to the rate of absorption. However, at higher light levels, excitation is approximately proportional to the logarithm of the rate of absorption, so if the vertical axis were relabeled Excitation, the correct curves would look somewhat different. The R and G curves would rise less steeply, and the B curve would approximately double in height relative to the R and G curves.

The absorption spectrum of *rods* is not plotted in figure 10.3. A rod can signal the absorption of a single photon, but cones require more than one absorption. If the vertical axis of figure 10.3 were presented as the probability of an incident photon triggering a visual response and a rod absorption spectrum were included, the rod curve would be far above the cones. (Except that at the extreme long-wavelength end of the plots, the sensitivity of the R cones actually exceeds the rod sensitivity. That's why, under very dim illumination, objects, like some roses for example, look red while everything else looks colorless.)

Although it seems counterintuitive, the statistical properties of the arrival of photons at low light levels are such that requiring two photons instead of one to be absorbed in the same receptor within about a tenth of a second reduces the sensitivity of the system not by a factor of two but by a factor of 102,000! (That astonishing statistic is derived by Robert Rodieck, via Simeon Poisson [1781–1840], in his book *The First Steps in Seeing* [Sinauer and Associates, 1998]. If you are interested in a detailed discussion of this and some of the other topics in the present book, you will find Rodieck's book excellent.)

If a person's retinas contain only rods, they will be completely wavelength-blind. Signals from their retinas would vary along only one dimension, regardless of wavelength. In very dim light, all of us are wavelength-blind because the light is not intense enough to activate cones.

Now suppose someone had retinas containing only rods and G cones. In dim light, they would be wavelength-blind because only the rods would be operating. In moderate and brighter light, they would still be wavelength-blind, because the rods would stop contributing to vision, and although the G cones would send signals that varied with the wavelength and the rate of the absorbed photons, those signals would be wavelength-blind for exactly the same reasons as rods are wavelength-blind: the outputs of their cone system would vary along only one dimension. That person couldn't tell ripe from unripe bananas. However, as will be explained below, for a person with more than one cone system, the two would always be distinguishable. That kind of fact probably provided a strong basis for the evolution of eyes containing more than one cone type. (The existence of people with only one kind of cone is hypothetical. If there are such people, they must be extremely rare. That condition is discussed here just to help in developing an understanding of normal color vision.)

For the following discussion, assume that the light levels are high enough that the outputs of the rods can be neglected. Consider a person who has two but only two types of cones, say R and G. (The absence of the B cone system, called tritanopia, occurs in less than 0.03 percent of the population.)

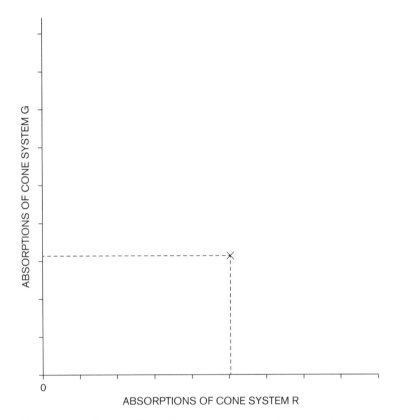

Figure 10.4. The two-dimensional space representing a visual system with two kinds of cones.

When light falls on that person's retina, the result can be represented in two dimensions, as in figure 10.4. The effect of a light of some intensity and wavelength composition will produce some rate of absorption in the R system, that is, along the horizontal axis, and some other rate in the G system, along the vertical axis. That is, the effect of any light can be represented by some point in this two-dimensional space. Any spot of light that would cause either or both the R and G systems to have a different rate of absorption would be plotted at a different point in this space, would cause a different combination of excitations, and would therefore look different. Ripe and unripe bananas would look different no matter the light level. (That doesn't just work for bananas. It works for anything where color matters.)

Suppose two spots of different wavelength compositions are displayed next to each other. There is no single adjustment to the intensities illuminating the spots that would cause their representations to coincide, that is to make the spots indistinguishable. However, if one of the spots contained a mixture of two wavelengths and you could adjust the intensities of both wavelengths, you could make the two spots look identical. Figure 10.5 is an example. If the lights represented by *a* and *b* are adjusted in intensity and added, their sum causes a number of absorptions in the R and the G systems that can be plotted anywhere in the space between the two outer diagonal lines, that is, the addition can exactly match any other mixture that is plotted there, such as the mixture in figure 10.4. If someone has two and only two cone systems (with overlapping but different absorption spectra), there are many combinations of lights that are physically different but that look identical.

For a person with retinas containing only rods or rods and only one type of cones, when two spots are presented next to each other, they can be made to appear identical by making only one adjustment, changing the intensity or the wavelength on either spot. If the retina contains two cone types, one adjustment will not be sufficient but two can be. There are objects in the world that differ in the composition of wavelengths they reflect but whose effects can be plotted at the same point in this two-dimensional space and that therefore look identical to a person with only two types of cones.

If the light represented in figure 10.4 is reduced in intensity, the absorption of both cone systems will be reduced by the same proportion, so the representative point will move along the diagonal line from the point plotted in figure 10.4 toward the origin. As will be discussed extensively later in this chapter, the subject would report this change as a change in "brightness," but the color, the "hue," depends on the relationship between the excitations of the two cone systems and so would

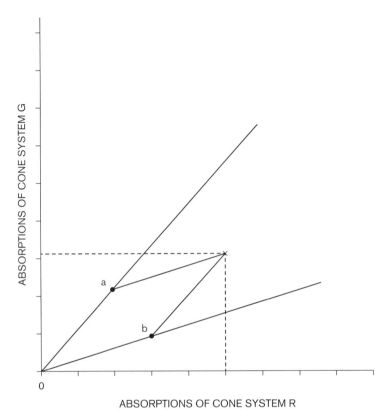

Figure 10.5. Light from two different wavelengths or mixtures of wavelengths can be found (points *a* and *b*) that, when added together, match another light (point *x*).

remain the same. (That is not exactly true. The hues of most wavelengths do change slightly when their intensities are changed, probably because the logarithmic relationships between intensity and excitation are slightly different for the different cone types.) It is much easier to find pairs of adjustments in intensity that are represented somewhere along the diagonal line than to find ones that plot to the same point. That means that, for this person, the number of objects in the world that may appear to have different brightnesses but the same hue is enormously larger than the number that look identical.

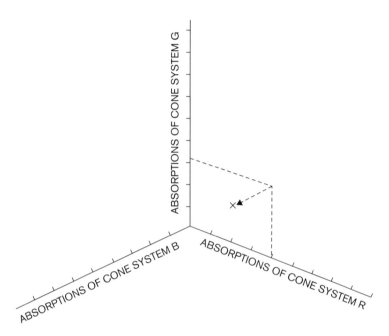

Figure 10.6. The three-dimensional space representing the effects of a light on a visual system containing all three cone types.

About 1.2 percent of men and about 0.2 percent of women have B and R cone systems but are missing the G cone system. (That is called deuteranopia.) All of the preceding discussion applies to them too, simply substituting the cone system labeled B for that labeled G.

"Normal" retinas contain cones with three different absorption spectra. Their responses to lights of various wavelengths and intensities can therefore be represented in a three-dimensional space as, for example, the *x* in figure 10.6. For a person with three cone systems that differ in their absorption spectra, that is, people with normal vision, if any two regions reflecting different wavelengths happen to be represented by the same point in two-dimensional space, they probably differ in the third dimension, and so will almost always look different.

SO WHY HAVE WE EVOLVED THREE RATHER THAN JUST TWO PIGMENTS?

The preceding sentence says "*almost* always." As described above, if a person has only one type of active receptor, that person will be wavelength-blind. If the person has two kinds of active receptors differing in their absorption spectra, the person will no longer be wavelength-blind. However, for that person, it is possible to find combinations of two (or more) wavelengths at the right intensities in one patch that will appear identical to any other wavelength or combination of wavelengths in another patch, and it is even easier to find combinations that are represented along the same diagonal line to the origin, that is, as explained below, they have different brightnesses but the same hue.

Similarly, if a person's retina contains receptors with three different absorption spectra, it will be possible (but a lot harder) to find a combination of the intensities of three (or more) wavelengths that will look identical or of the same hue as any other wavelength or mixture. In general, the more different kinds of absorption spectra, the harder it is (and the rarer it is in nature) to find two regions differing in wavelength composition that look identical or that cannot be distinguished by their hues.

THEN WHY HAVEN'T WE EVOLVED MORE THAN THREE KINDS OF CONES?

Consider the factors that have shaped the evolution of the rods and cones in the human. Most primitive animals, for example most reptiles, have no rod system and so cannot see at night. The evolution of rods, then, provided an important advantage. If early humans evolved a rod system in addition to one cone system, they would have the added advantage of vision in dim light but would still be wavelength-blind. Having more than one cone system with somewhat different absorption spectra would provide the important ability to distinguish objects by hue as well as brightnesses. There is a lot more information in a color photograph than in a grayscale one.

Virtually all natural light contains a broad mixture of different wavelengths at different intensities. No matter how many different wavelengths fall on a patch of normal retina, there will always be three and only three different groups of signals indicating the wavelength mixture, one from each of the three cone types, because once photons are absorbed in a cone, the output of that cone signals only the fact of the absorption, the wavelength information having been lost. Almost always, regions reflecting different combinations of wavelengths will produce different combinations of the three kinds of cone signals and will therefore look different.

Suppose a scene presents just two disks of light. As discussed above, for a person with only one class of cones, it is easy to adjust the intensity of either disk until the two disks look identical regardless of their wavelengths. Similarly, and probably more importantly for the evolution of the visual system, it would be easy for this person to confuse two foods, for example ripe and unripe bananas, that would always appear different to a person with normal vision. For a person with two classes of cones, the set of objects that actually differ but appear identical is greatly reduced, but not entirely eliminated. It would still be possible to mix lights of different wavelengths and intensities in such a way that although two disks are physically different, they both produce the same pair of excitations from the two cone systems and so would look identical. Adding a third cone system reduces the set of indistinguishable combinations of wavelengths still further.

In nature there are very few examples of things that reflect different combinations of visible wavelengths but are indistinguishable to a person with normal vision, so evolutionary "forces" that favor more than three cone types are weak. But there are two examples, found in almost every home but not in "nature": color television and computer screens. If you examine such a screen under high magnification, you will discover that it consists of a large array of only three (or sometimes four) kinds of tiny dots, each of which emits a different color or small group of wavelengths, usually red, green, or blue. Yet when viewed at an ordinary distance, so that the images of the individual dots are so close together on the retina that they overlap, that is, mix, the colors of objects on the screen match almost all of the colors in a real scene. Ripe bananas are yellow, leaves are green. The proper adjustments of the intensities of just three different sets of wavelengths, the tiny dots, can duplicate the visual effects of almost all the mixtures of wavelengths and intensities in the world.

The extremely limited range of electromagnetic wavelengths that humans can sense was discussed in chapter 1. Even within that limited range, our visual systems have managed to develop receptor systems that use different sub-ranges to detect significant information. But why is the range so restricted? Would it be of advantage to be able to sense much shorter or longer wavelengths?

Some animals, for example bees, can detect short wavelengths in what is called the ultraviolet, but the earth's atmosphere absorbs so much of the ultraviolet light from the sun that sensing it would rarely be useful to humans. It might seem useful for us to be able to sense extremely short wavelengths such as X-rays—certainly the X-ray devices that technology has created are useful. But to make an X-ray image, the X-rays must be created by man-made devices; natural sources of X-rays, such as radium, are rare, and if they were not rare, we would have had to evolve tissues and genes that are not so easily destroyed by the extremely high energy that each X-ray quantum contains.

Man-made devices are now available that can detect and form images using light of wavelengths just a little longer than the visible wavelengths. That region of the spectrum is called infrared. The electrons that are constantly moving in matter generate electromagnetic waves in the infrared region of the spectrum, and the faster they move, that is, the higher the temperature of the matter, the greater the number of infrared photons that are emitted. That is the basis of many security cameras that are now available. They form images from the infrared light emitted by cars and people. But since living tissues emit infrared light, so does the eyeball itself. Therefore, if our eyes contained infrared receptors, they would be constantly flooded by self-generated infrared and so would not be useful. (It is certainly useful for some cold-blooded animals to be able to sense infrared photons, animals that prey on or are preyed upon by warm-blooded animals.)

COLOR NAMES

The light from the sun and from most lightbulbs contains photons with a broad range of wavelengths, so when it falls on the retina, all three kinds of cones are activated. When roughly equal signals are produced by the three kinds of receptors, we have learned to call that experience *white* in English, *blanc* in French, *blanco* in Spanish, and so on. When the photons all have wavelengths of about 575 nm, the G and R photoreceptors are activated about equally, and the B receptors very weakly. We have learned to call that particular pattern of excitations yellow. Wavelengths longer than that are called red or reddish; wavelengths in the middle produce patterns of excitation that we call green; short wavelengths are called blue. That is, people with normal vision have been taught to call by different names different combinations of activity of the three types of cones.

Now we can try to answer a question that is asked often: "What colors do color-blind people see?" If that is a question about how a person with color blindness *experiences* colors, it cannot be answered sensibly. How would *you* describe your experience of color? When asked about sensory experiences, we answer with comparisons to other experiences. "The sky looks like it's on fire." "This wine has hints of cherry." But in an important way, the names themselves given to colors are descriptions of experiences. For example, look at a clear sky in daylight. Saying it looks blue *is* a description of your experience. So the preceding discussion of the mechanisms of color vision and the following discussion of color names do provide a form of answers to the question.

People missing one of the normal pigments are often called color-blind. It is likely that color-blind people have the same brain mechanisms as normal people do and the same excitation patterns traveling to the brain, except that the contribution of one of the pigments is simply missing. Therefore, the color a color-blind person sees or at least reports seeing is probably predictable. Suppose a person has no R pigment and a light of 575 nm falls on their retinas. The retinas would send signals to the brain, but although the pattern of signals would be missing the R component, it still would consist of a set of relative strengths from the G and B systems. The retinas of this person, missing the R cone pigment, would send a pattern of signals to the brain that is similar to the pattern in a person with normal color vision when the retina of the normal person is illuminated with a light at 550 nm. Most people with normal color vision and speaking English call the pattern of excitations from light at 550 nm green, so the color-blind person would probably have learned, from people with normal color vision, that the pattern arriving in their brains at 575 nm is called green. Similarly, if a person is missing the G cones, they have probably learned to call a light at 575 nm red.

In elementary school we are taught about color in terms of "color wheels," "color triangles," and similar words and diagrams that relate to the appearances of mixtures of wavelengths. Those terms and diagrams are widely used by people involved in art and design, and they refer to three different aspects of the appearance of spots of light. These three aspects are difficult to define precisely because they are subjective, but they can be distinguished by reference to the physical characteristics of the corresponding light falling on the retina, as follows.

Brightness is what you expect it to mean, the aspect that changes when the intensity of the light, the number of photons per second, changes. *Hue* is the aspect that changes when the wavelength of the light changes. *Saturation* is the aspect that changes if the breadth of the spectrum of light changes, so a light of just one wavelength, for instance the light emitted by a red laser pointer, is highly saturated, but if it is mixed with white light so it becomes pink, it is said to be less saturated.

Because normal vision is enabled by three different sets of cones, R, G, and B, every spot of light on the retina sends a set of signals to the brain that can vary in three dimensions. The experiences of brightness, hue, and saturation are entirely based on the patterns of those signals.

Now reconsider the physiology of color vision in terms of subjective appearances. Suppose a person has only one kind of cone. That person's experiences of light vary in only one way, that is, along only one dimension, as shown in figure 10.7. No matter what wavelength or combination of wavelengths is arriving at each point on the retina, the signals from that person's retina just get stronger or weaker, depending on the total rate of absorption of photons. (The x in the figure would move horizontally.) They would see only differences in "brightness." Because people with normal vision have only one kind of signal in very dim light, from rods, and the "colors" that people with normal color vision usually report under those conditions are shades of gray, this one-kind-of-cone person would probably have been taught to call all wavelengths and mixtures of wavelengths shades of gray.)

0

PHOTON ABSORPTIONS

Figure 10.7. A copy of figure 10.2: the effects of light on a visual system containing only one active kind of receptor.

Suppose you present a disk of light to this person who has only rods. You set the intensity at, say, 1,000 photons per second per square millimeter and the wavelength at 350 nm, and then smoothly turn a knob to increase the wavelength, keeping the intensity constant. Initially, at 350 nm, the subject would see only darkness, and the response would be plotted at zero, in figure 10.7. When the wavelength got to about 400 nm, the response would begin to move above zero. It would continue to move to the right until the wavelength produced maximum absorption, then move back toward the origin. The effect on the visual system could only change

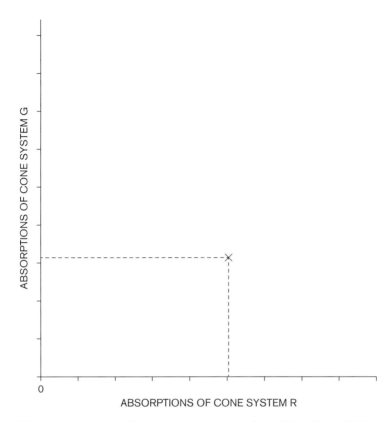

Figure 10.8. A copy of figure 10.4: a representation of the effect of light of a particular intensity and wavelength on a visual system with two cone systems. The effect varies in two dimensions.

along one dimension, and the subject would describe the appearance as changing in brightness. If you stayed with a particular wavelength and changed its intensity, the plotted point would also move horizontally, and the subject would also say its brightness changed. So that person's visual experience can be described as only changing in brightness.

Now consider a person with two kinds of cones, say R and G, for example. Their retinas deliver two signals, one depending only on the total rate of excitation of the R cones and the other on the total rate of excitation of the G cones, so their color vision varies in two dimensions,

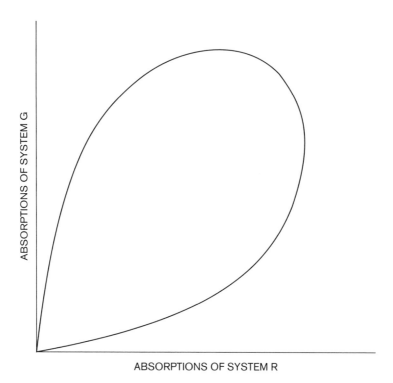

Figure 10.9. The effect of a light of fixed intensity on a visual system with two kinds of cones, as the wavelength is varied.

as represented by the space between axes in figure 10.8. As discussed above, for this person, any wavelength or combination of wavelengths can be completely represented by one point in two-dimensional space. An example point is plotted in figure 10.8.

Suppose you again display an illuminated disk with a fixed intensity, say 1,000 photons per second, and smoothly change the wavelength from very short to very long. The points representing the effects will move along the curve in figure 10.9. At very long wavelengths, the effect on the R cones will be a lot stronger than the effect on the G cones, but as the wavelength changes, the relationship between the two excitations will change, and the subject's experience will change along two

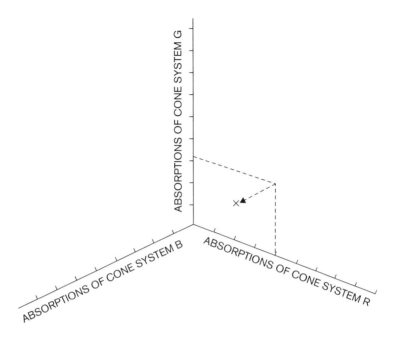

Figure 10.10. A copy of figure 10.6: the effect of a light of a particular intensity and wavelength on a visual system with three kinds of cones.

dimensions. They will probably call the change in the angle between the point and the origin a change in hue, and the change in distance from the origin a change in brightness. And, since if you change the intensity of the illumination the plotted point will move away from the origin, they will call that a change in brightness too.

Normal color vision is enabled by three different sets of cones, and so the effect of any combination of wavelengths can be plotted as a point somewhere in three-dimensional space, as in figure 10.10. The *x* indicates the effects of one spot of light. Imagine this three-dimensional volume filled with color names, light bright pink, dark blue-green, and so on. Think of this 3-space as the corner of a room where two walls meet the floor, and imagine a line coming out diagonally from the corner toward the middle of the room so that each point along the line is an equal distance from each of the two walls and from the floor. Each point along that line represents the effect of a light that is about equally strongly absorbed by all three cone types. A disk of light on a dark background with an effect that would be plotted as a point on that line, say one foot from the corner, would be called gray. If the intensity of the light increased, moving the corresponding point along that line farther from the corner, the disk would be called lighter gray. Its *brightness* would increase, but its hue and saturation would not change. If, instead, the wavelength composition of the light falling on the retina were changed so that the representative point moved in any direction away from the diagonal line, the *saturation* would change, for example from light gray to pink to red. And if the ratios of excitations among the three cone systems changed, so that the point moved in a circular path around the diagonal, grey-to-white line, the *hue* would change.

This mapping of color is not exactly what actually happens, but it is close. For instance, if the intensities of all the wavelengths illuminating a spot are increased by the same proportion—say all double—the plotted spot will move away from the corner along the diagonal line from the point to the corner, and the brightness of the stimulus will increase, but its hue will also change a little. (It would not change at all if the outputs of the three different kinds of receptors were related to the rates of their absorption by exactly the same perfect logarithmic function, but the relationship is not quite logarithmic and may differ a little among cone types.)

As mentioned at the beginning of this chapter, the hue of an extremely bright red light changes in a few seconds from red through yellow to green, and then slowly back to orange. Referring back to figure 7.1 (p. xxx), which showed that at very high intensities, the rates of bleaching actually cross, those changes in hue make sense. Initially, the R system has the highest rate of bleaching; after a second or two, the R and G systems have equal bleaching rates, producing yellow; next, for a while the rate of bleaching of the G system is greatest; and finally the rate of the R system becomes greatest again.

The idea of *saturation* in this kind of plot is also complicated. The (subjective) judgement of saturation is partly dependent on wavelength.

For example, most people will say that a spot illuminated only at a wavelength of 575 nm appears yellow and a spot at 700 nm is red, but they will also say that the 575 nm spot is less saturated than the 700 nm spot, even when both are as far away from the center line as they can get.

COLOR CONSTANCY

The phenomenon called color constancy is frequently discussed in the vision literature, but there seem to be three different definitions of that term. One states that color constancy refers to the fact that hues of objects change very little under changes in their illumination. That definition does not specify whether the "changes in illumination" are changes in intensity or in wavelength composition, or both. Another definition refers to the fact that hue changes very little when the *intensity* of its illumination changes, and a third definition refers to the change or lack of change in hue when the *wavelength* composition of the illumination changes. The physiology underlying the effects of changes in illumination intensity is different from that underlying the effects of changes in illuminant wavelength composition, so it would be best to disregard the first definition and to assign different names to the phenomena referred to by the second and third definitions.

Let's call the phenomenon in which hue changes very little when the intensity of the illumination varies HI (hue intensity) constancy and the other HW (hue wavelength-composition) constancy and discuss them separately. (Among people doing vision research, two scenes are said to differ in "color" if they differ in hue *or brightness or saturation,* so it is better to substitute "hue" for "color" in these labels.)

HI Constancy

Suppose you are looking at a flag that consists of red and green stripes. When a shadow falls on the flag, reducing the illumination falling on it by, say, a factor of ten, the stripes still look red and green. Although the excitations of the three color systems in your eyes have all changed, the ratios among those excitations have not changed. As discussed in chapter 6 regarding brightness constancy, a logarithmic relationship between intensity and excitation is one that produces a ratio of excitation that does not change with intensity. Therefore, for exactly the same reasons as were discussed in chapter 6, a logarithmic relationship between intensity and excitation also explains HI constancy.

HW Constancy

The illumination on most scenes—sunlight, light from a lightbulb, and so on—consists of a broad range of different wavelengths. Surfaces that vary in hue do so because the molecules in them absorb different proportions of different wavelengths, just as the visual pigments in the receptors do. As a result, the wavelength composition of the light reflected from them is different from the incident wavelength composition. If the wavelength composition of the incident light changes, the composition of the reflected light must change as well, and so, in fact, when the composition of the illuminating light first changes, the hues of the illuminated objects change too; the hues are *not* constant. Further, if the illumination changes strongly, say from sunlight to laser light, that is, from a broad spectrum to a very narrow one, the hues of objects also must change and HW constancy does not occur.

However, if the wavelength composition of the illumination changes mildly, as, for example, when going from a reading lamp to sunlight, then after a second or two, the hues of objects are essentially the same as they were before the wavelength composition of the illuminant changed. Under those restricted conditions, HW constancy does hold, and can be easily understood when the processes of light and dark adaptation are considered. For example, suppose the long-wavelength component of the illumination increases relative to the other wavelengths, as it might as the sun sets. The absorption of photons by the R cone system will increase relative to the G and B systems. Therefore, over the next second or two the relative sensitivity of the R system will be reduced, partially compensating for the increase in the long wavelengths. Although such adaptation cannot completely compensate, if the change in illuminant wavelength is not too strong, the resulting change in hue may be too small to notice.

THINGS TO THINK ABOUT

1. Some fruits change color when ripe. Others don't. What might be the evolutionary advantages of changing color when ripe? (It is much harder than it might look at first to give a complete answer to this question.)

2. How would you find out whether or not your cousin is color-blind? (This is also a very hard question to answer properly.)

3. How would you find out whether or not your goldfish is color-blind? (This is maybe even harder.)

4. Two patches of light are presented side by side, both at the same wavelength but one at twice the intensity of the other. A subject with normal color vision will report that the hues of the two patches are slightly different. (The change in hue with intensity is called the Bezold-Brücke effect.) What mechanisms might explain the change in hue? (Hint: Absorption spectra like those in figure 10.3 represent the probability that photons of the various wavelengths will be absorbed by a *thin layer* of pigment, but each receptor in the human eye is a tube, so a photon passing through the top layer still has a lot of chances of being absorbed by lower layers.)

   According to the absorption spectra in figure 10.3, the probabilities of absorption by the R and the G pigments are equal at 575 nm, which might lead to the expectation that there should be no change in hue with intensity at that wavelength; and, in fact, it has often been stated that the Bezold-Brücke effect is zero at 575 nm. However, that is not correct. With careful measurement, it is clear that hue *does* change with intensity at 575 nm (Robert E.

Savoie, "Bezold-Brücke Effect and Visual Nonlinearity," *Journal of the American Optical Society* 63 [1973]: 1253–61). What might explain the hue shifts at 575 nm? (Hint: The absorption of photons does not directly affect the strength of the signal in the optic nerves. There are several neural stages between the pigment and the optic nerves.)

RELEVANT READING

T. N. Cornsweet, H. Fowler, R. G. Rabedeau, R. E. Whalen, and D. R. Williams. 1958. "Changes in the Perceived Color of Very Bright Stimuli." *Science* 128: 898–99.

CHAPTER ELEVEN

Actually Seeing and Not Seeing

Neural Mechanisms

It was discovered about a century ago that even if you try to hold your gaze steady, your eyes are always in motion. For example, look at the point in the very center of the disk in figure II.I. To do that, as explained in chapter 8, your eye rotates, causing your retina to slide under the image of the dot so that the image falls on a particular region near the center of the retina, the fovea.

Even if you try to hold your gaze on the point as steadily as you can, your eyes will constantly undergo small rotational movements so your retinas will continuously slide around under the image. The area inside the dots surrounding the point at the center in figure II.I indicates the average size of the shifting, or the average area of the retina that the image of the point moves across during each second when an average person is trying to fixate steadily and the page is about one foot away from the eye.

The publications of the first accurate measurements of this continuous motion generated an active debate regarding its causes and its effects on vision. Some groups asserted that the motion must spoil vision, while others claimed that it was beneficial. It turned out that both views are correct. The smaller the motion, the better the acuity, but in the complete absence of motion, vision fails completely.

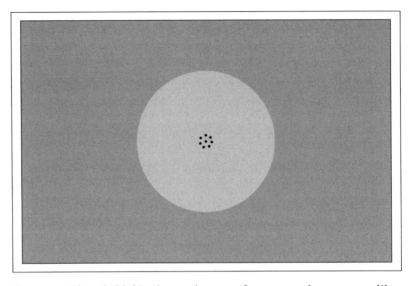

Figure 11.1. If you hold this picture about one foot away and stare as steadily as you can at the dot in the very center, no matter how carefully you try to keep your gaze steady, your eyes will continuously move so that the retinal image of the central dot will move around in a region approximately the size indicated by the small circle of dots around the central one.

The study of these small eye movements has led to the recognition of some surprising, profound, and fundamental visual processes. To understand these processes it is helpful, first, to consider how the measurements that led to that understanding were made.

The eye rotates about a point roughly in the center of the eyeball, which is about half an inch behind the cornea and half an inch in front of the retina. During a typical attempt at steady fixation, the continuous rotations of the eye cause actual translational movement of the cornea (and the retina in the opposite direction) of only about a thousandth of an inch, so accurate measurements are not easy.

One technique used in an early attempt to measure tiny eye movements involved putting a small drop of mercury on the cornea (before it was understood that mercury is poisonous), which, when illuminated, reflected a tiny bright dot. The dot was then greatly magnified and its motion was recorded photographically. That procedure provided nice measurements of the movement of the mercury but failed to indicate the motion of the retinal image with respect to the retina. It measured the translation of the dot, but, as explained in chapter 8, so long as the scene is more than a foot or so away from the eye, translations cause only negligible motion of the retinal image with respect to the retina. It is rotations of the eye that slide the retina under the retinal image.

A technique that is unaffected by translations of the eye but measures rotations was then developed. In the early and mid-twentieth century, contact lenses were large and covered most of the front of the eyeball. (These "scleral lenses" are still used to treat certain pathologies.) After performing a refraction, an ophthalmologist or optometrist applied a drop to anesthetize the cornea and made a mold of the front of the eye by covering it with a liquid that gelled in a few minutes to a rubber-like material and then was easily peeled off. The mold was sent to a facility that formed a contact lens, out of plastic, that fit the mold on the back (corneal) side and had the correct curvature on the front side to satisfy the results of the refraction. To wear the lens, it was held horizontally, to form a cup, and filled with a solution compounded for the purpose. The user then moved the eye downwards and into the fluid filling the lens, and pressed a little to ensure that the fit was tight, a procedure that took a lot of practice and patience, and sometimes tolerance for pain.

For use in measuring tiny eye movements, a small flat mirror was glued to the outside of the contact lens, to the side of the line of sight, as in figure 11.2. A small hole was drilled through the lens on the other side of the line of sight, and the hole was covered with a small piece of adhesive tape. The lens was then pressed firmly against the eyeball so that it fitted tightly. (To remove the lens, the tape was pulled off, breaking the suction that held the lens on.) Then, to record the horizontal rotation of the eye, the subject, using the eye wearing the contact lens, looked at a target, and an optical assembly similar to a slide projector projected light onto the mirror in such a way that the reflected light formed the

Figure 11.2. A scleral contact lens with a small flat mirror mounted on it, like that initially used to measure very small eye movements.

image of a bright spot on a strip of photographic paper that was continuously moving vertically. That way, if the eye rotated horizontally, the bright point moved horizontally across the moving paper. (The optical system included a component that prevented vertical movements from affecting the recording.) Afterward, the long strip of photographic paper was developed and the trace measured with a ruler. When the distance between the mirror and the photographic paper was large, the light reflected from the mirror acted as a large "lever arm" to magnify the effect of the rotation of the eye, but translating the (flat) mirror did not affect the recording.

The reason for describing all of that is that when the subject is in the apparatus, he can see the bright spot, and it moves back and forth when his eye moves back and forth, triggering the idea that it might be possible to allow the eye to move normally but to make the retinal image move too, in such a way that there is no motion between the retina and the retinal image.

The measurement setup described above won't quite do it. The problem is that when a mirror rotates through some angle, the reflected light moves through twice the angle. So if the subject in the apparatus, wearing the contact lens with the mirror on it, rotates his eye so that he is looking, say, one inch to the right, the reflected light will move two inches to the right, so the retinal image will still move with respect to the retina. To correct that problem, the light reflected from the mirror was made to follow a path exactly twice as long as the path through which the subject saw the target directly. That way, the retinal image of the reflected light moved through exactly the same distance (and direction) as the retina moved: the image was "stabilized" on the retina. Under those conditions, in a fraction of a second the stabilized target simply disappeared. The word "exactly" was purposely used twice in the preceding description. Even a very tiny movement of the image with respect to the retina is sufficient to briefly restore the visibility of the target, so the instrumentation has to prevent that movement exactly. (By now, several different ways to measure tiny eye movements and to stabilize images have been developed that do not require any attachments to the eye.)

WHAT DOES IT MEAN TO SAY THE TARGET DISAPPEARED?

It is fairly easy to imagine a neural circuit that transmits only changing signals and therefore causes a stabilized image to disappear. An example of a circuit that does that will be discussed later. The existence of such a circuit in the visual system would seem to explain the disappearance, but in fact it does not. For instance, suppose the target reflected from the mirror is a bright disk on a gray background. If there is no response unless the light level on receptors is changing, when the disk disappears it should turn black. Stabilized images do not turn black. If the bright disk turned black, it would not disappear, it would become a black disk (on a gray background). The actual meaning of the *disappearance* of stabilized images is fundamental to the understanding of almost all visual

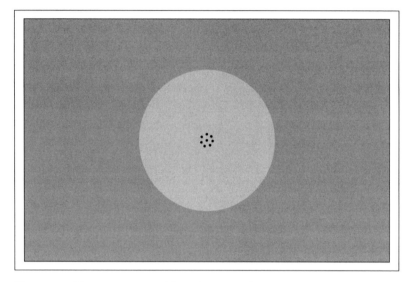

Figure 11.3. Figure 11.1 repeated here for convenience.

phenomena, but to clarify that meaning, what will appear to be a side-track needs to be examined; the physical properties of the stabilizing apparatus need to be carefully considered.

In general, to stabilize an image there must be a device that measures the movements of the eye and another, for example a computer-driven screen, that presents a stimulus pattern to the subject which moves in exact accordance with their eye movements. But the field of view of a human eye extends almost 90 degrees left and right, and arranging a stabilized display that large would be extraordinarily difficult. So a stimulus pattern that moves with the eye cannot extend to fill the subject's entire visual field; it must have visible edges. That is, it must have borders that do not move with the eye and therefore cannot be stabilized.

Figure 11.3 is a copy of figure 11.1. Consider the rectangle as the frame of a computer monitor. If the light-gray disk and the points in its center were stabilized, the disk and center points would disappear. That is, the appearance of the scene would be of a uniform dark-gray space inside the frame. In fact, if the disk were stabilized, the scene would appear to be a uniform dark-gray space regardless of the brightness and color of the disk. The brightness and color of the space inside the frame would depend *only on the change in brightness and color at the inside borders of the rectangle.* It would just look like a dark-gray rectangle.

As another example, imagine a display in which a red disk is centered on a square green background. If the image of the red disk is stabilized on the retina, it will rapidly disappear, and the scene will appear as a uniform green square.

When you try to look as steadily as possible at the dot in the center of figure 11.3 without any special apparatus, your eye movements will cause the image to shift continuously over a region about the size indicated by the dotted region surrounding the central dot. That means that the whole image of the disk will also shift around with respect to the retina over about the same small distance, and the disk and the points in the center of it will remain visible. However, because the region of shifting is so small, most of the photoreceptors—all but those lying under a narrow ring around the circumference of the disk—will *undergo no changes in illumination.* They will have no way of "knowing" whether the disk is stabilized or not. Similarly, because the movements are so small, receptors under almost all of the area between the disk and the border will also be presented with an unchanging light intensity. That means that the receptors under most of the area of the disk *and* most of the area outside the disk will undergo unchanging stimulation! The only regions of the retina that will be affected by movements of the eye will be areas very near the borders, the places where eye movements change the intensities falling on neighboring receptors. But under normal viewing, when eye movements cause slight movements of the image across the receptors, figure 11.3 doesn't look at all like that would lead you to expect. It doesn't look like a narrow ring. It looks like a gray disk on a darker gray rectangular background, with some spots in the middle.

The natural world looks like we would expect it to look, as long as we constantly make small eye movements that we don't normally even

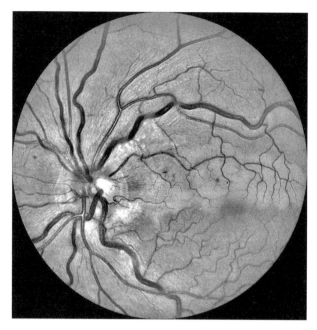

Figure 11.4. Another photograph of an ocular fundus.

know about. But once we know that stabilized images disappear, we might expect that every fairly uniformly lighted region in every scene should look identical with every other uniformly lighted region. We should only see places where the intensity in the retinal image is changing. We should see only *borders*.

But things are even more confusing than that. Figure 11.4 is another image of the retinal blood vessels. (Do you notice a few dark dots in this image? They are tiny bleeds, early symptoms of diabetic retinopathy. The whitish lines that form a sort of texture are groups of optic nerve fibers running over the surface of the retina to exit the eyeball at the optic disk and form the optic nerve.) The blood vessels always cast strong shadows on almost all of the retina, yet they are only visible under the special conditions that were discussed in chapter 5. Because the vessels are attached to the retina and move with it, their shadows are "stabilized," so their disappearance might be expected. But in fact

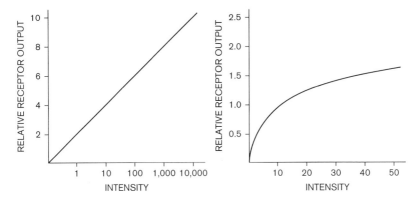

Figure 11.5. Two ways to plot a logarithmic relationship between the intensity of light falling on a region of the retina and the resulting strength of excitation. Note that the scaling of the axes is different but both represent a logarithmic relationship.

their lack of appearance reveals another, major, puzzle. Blood vessels are not completely opaque. They transmit some fixed proportion of the incident light, so the intensity under their shadows depends on the intensity of the light incident on them. Every time we look from one place to another, unless the two places happen to reflect exactly the same amount of light, the amount of light falling on both the inside and the outside of every retinal blood-vessel shadow will change, just as it would if the shadow actually moved with respect to the receptors. Yet the shadows remain invisible.

The relationship between the intensity of light falling on a receptor and the strength of its output has been discussed in several places earlier in this book. As a reminder, figure 11.5 shows this general relationship again. Both curves represent the same relationship; they only differ in the way the scaling of the horizontal axis is presented. Both show that the output of a receptor is approximately proportional to the logarithm of the intensity of light falling on it. Brightness constancy is one result. That relationship will be referred to again in the following discussion.

Given that the signal sent to the brain by each receptor and its neural connections is proportional not to the intensity falling on it but approximately to the logarithm of the intensity, then the description of what is happening as the result of an eye movement changes in a major way. Although it is still true that looking from one place to another will cause the intensities at the inside and outside of a blood-vessel shadow to change, their *ratio* will not change. (This is obviously closely related to brightness constancy.) So if the apparent brightness of a region of the scene depends not simply on borders but on changes in the ratio of the intensities falling on neighboring receptors, then it makes sense that blood-vessel shadows should remain invisible when we look from place to place. The apparent brightness (and hue) of each place in a scene depends on changes in the ratios of intensities that occur at borders during eye movements, and those ratios, at the edges of the shadows of blood vessels, do not change during eye movements.

If that is true—and the evidence strongly supports that statement—then why do we *ever* see blood-vessel shadows? Under some of the conditions described in chapter 5 that allow us to see blood-vessel shadows, the amount of light falling on the receptors changes between some level in the normal range of vision and another level that is extremely low. Under those conditions, that is, when the intensity of light falling on receptors suddenly becomes close to zero, the logarithmic relationship breaks down. So when, for instance, you look at a bright area of the sky and alternately let the light fall on your retina briefly and then block it, the ratios of intensities at the borders of blood-vessel shadows will not be constant. If the light level under the shadow is taken as the numerator, the ratio approaches zero when the light is blocked, and if the ratio is taken with the light level as the denominator, it will approach infinity. It is this failure of the maintenance of ratios that lets us see retinal blood-vessel shadows when, for instance, we block and briefly unblock light.

Seeing blood-vessel shadows when looking through a pinhole that is moving, or when moving a small spot of light on the sclera as in figure 5.4 (p. xxx), can be explained by a different process. Figure 11.6 is a

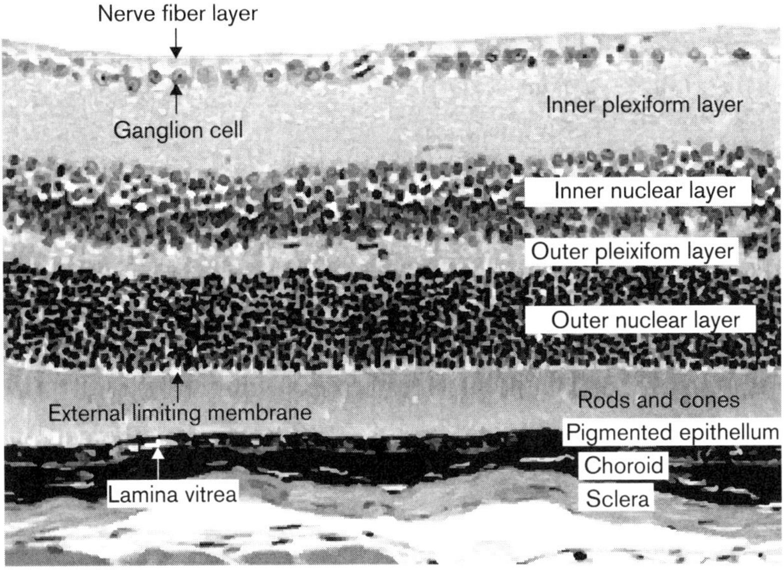

Figure 11.6. A stained and greatly magnified section through the retina, showing the different neural layers.

photograph, taken through a microscope, of a cross-section of the retina. The sample has been stained so that different kinds of cells appear in different shades of gray. At the very bottom is the sclera, the "white of the eye," and above that is layer mostly containing blood vessels, called the choroid. The vessels in the choroid are not the ones that cast shadows on the receptors; they supply the receptors with oxygen and other nutrients from below. Next is a layer of dark pigment, the pigmented epithelium, and above that is a layer of photoreceptors, rods and cones.

Skipping to the very top, the inner surface of the retina contains optic nerve fibers and ganglion cells. (The jelly-like vitreous humor lies above that.) The ganglion cells are the cell bodies of the nerve fibers that gather together to form the optic nerve and carry signals to the brain. (Those are the nerve fibers, or groups of fibers, visible in figure 11.4 as a texture of fine lines heading for the optic disk.) The blood vessels so visible in figure 11.4 lie on the surface of that top layer, so those vessels cast shadows on the receptors, the rods and cones. Further, there is a small but finite distance between those vessels and the photoreceptors, and that means that if you look through a moving pinhole or move small light on your sclera, the shadows will actually shift across the photoreceptors, producing changes in the light falling on them.

Another important message evident in figure 11.6 is that between the receptors and the nerve fiber layer are a number of layers (the number depends on how they are counted and who is doing the counting) containing various kinds of nerves and connections among nerves. A lot of processing of the signals from receptors goes on in those layers before the signals get to the optic nerve fibers, processing that strongly affects what we see. The processing that occurs in those layers underlies most of the effects involved in the disappearance and reappearance of stabilized images, and therefore underlies much of ordinary, unstabilized, vision.

The neural processes that control the disappearance of stabilized images and the appearance of unstabilized ones are complicated. Instead of simply converting light intensities into neural signal strengths and transmitting them to the brain, uniformly lighted regions all produce essentially the same excitation, edges are "extracted," changes in ratios of light levels are transmitted, and then, probably in a layer of the brain, those signals are processed to reconstruct patterns that correspond to the actual objects in the scene. Since this complicated set of steps has evolved in the human visual system, it seems likely that they contribute to survival in a significant way.

It is surely true in general that the more powerful an organism's memory, the less it needs to continuously monitor unchanging aspects of its environment. More specifically, because there is a limit to how fast neurons can fire, using a finite number of optic neurons to continuously deliver information about the structure of blood-vessel shadows and of the intensities of all the points in every uniformly illuminated region of the retinal image would interfere with the range and rate at which the optic nerve could deliver *more useful* information to the brain.

(And from a subjective point of view, for whatever that is worth, it would seem to be unpleasant to see the world always overlaid with blood-vessel shadows.)

Afterimages, both positive and negative, occur because during normal viewing, the distribution of intensities and wavelengths falling on the retina produces a corresponding distribution of adaptation, that is, differences in sensitivity, so each time the direction of gaze is shifted, an afterimage of the previous scene is superimposed on the new one. Afterimages are, in a sense, attached to the retina and so are stabilized and might be expected to disappear quickly. However, dark and light adaptation do take time, causing the strengths of afterimages to change, so if the changes are strong enough, afterimages are briefly visible. However, their changes in strength diminish quickly and are then overcome by the mechanisms that cause stabilized images to disappear. If afterimages did not disappear fairly quickly, the visual scene would constantly appear as the superposition of many shifted images.

EXPLANATIONS AND MODELS

The mechanisms involved in the disappearance of stabilized images, and therefore the mechanisms involved in vision in general, patched together by evolution, appear to be extremely complicated, and it is tempting simply to say that the brain figures out how to deal with signals from receptors to provide us with the information we need to survive, maybe by combining knowledge of the world with patterns of ongoing signals from receptors. Although that kind of "explanation" of visual phenomena can be found all too frequently in writings and television programs purporting to provide an understanding of vision, it does not constitute an explanation, just a rephrasing of the problem. Such "explanations" are not merely empty. They are harmful, because they delay and obfuscate the search for a proper understanding of our nervous system.

Chapter 6 consists of an extensive discussion about brightness constancy, a phenomenon that would seem to require a complex explanation

Figure 11.7. An illustration of the effect of the intensity of the background on brightness. The two inset squares reflect identical amounts of light. This is called a contrast effect.

but instead follows from a relatively simple process, the process that produces a logarithmic relationship between light intensity and receptor output. It is often possible to find relatively simple ways in which neural elements can interact that provide an explanation of other apparently complicated operations of the visual system, operations that cause the appearance of things in the world to agree with the physical properties of the things that are important for survival.

A large group of scenes display what are usually called illusions, that is, scenes with appearances that differ from their actual light distributions. (Brightness constancy might properly be called an illusion.) Figure 11.7 is a classic example. The two inset squares are physically identical shades of gray, that is, they both reflect the same percentage of incident light. The difference in their backgrounds, and the resulting neural interactions, produces the difference in their apparent brightnesses. This is actually another example of the fact that the brightness of a uniform area depends only on the differences in intensities at its edges.

Figure 11.8 is another, more complex, example. The squares labeled A and B are printed with exactly the same shade of gray as all of the "black" squares that are not in the shadow. (If you don't believe that, cut two small holes in something opaque so that square A shows through one hole and square B through the other. Then both squares will have the same surroundings and will appear equally light.) Note that the shadow of the tube is not sharply defined. It is the kind of shadow that is produced when the light source casting the shadow is wide. If the shadow is sharp,

Figure 11.8. Another example of a contrast effect. The squares labeled *A* and *B* reflect identical amounts of light. From Edward H. Adelson.

as it would be if the light source were small, then the illusion does not work.

It is compelling to try to explain this illusion by thinking something like: "One square lies in the shadow of the tube while the other doesn't. Our system recognizes the shadow and compensates for it, so we see the scene the way it really is in the world." But that's not really an explanation, it's just a rephrasing of the problem. *How* does our visual system compensate? What are the mechanisms that do that?

The patterns in figure 11.9 demonstrate two different forms of "illusion." The physical reflectances in the pattern on the right are simply what they look like. The center is a uniformly gray disk on a lighter background, as plotted in cross-section beneath it. The reflectances of the pattern on the left are different from the ones on the right. The

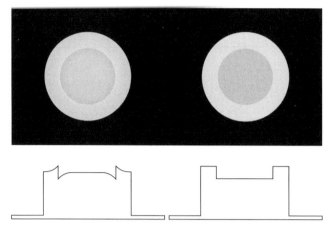

Figure 11.9. Two disks that look alike but are physically different. Plots of the actual amount of light reflected from each lie below them. This scene displays two different phenomena: one, that the two disks look alike although they actually differ; and two, that the brightnesses at the centers of both disks appear different from the brightnesses of their annuli rather than both centers appearing the same as their annuli.

disk and its background have identical reflectances, as plotted below. But in spite of their differences, the two (upper) patterns look almost alike.

There are two different aspects to this illusion. Both aspects are important, and each has a different explanation. The first aspect is that the two patterns are different but look alike. The second is that both look like what one would expect for the one on the right rather than both looking like the one on the left. The illusion in figure 11.9 is another illustration that the brightness of a region depends not on the intensity of its retinal illumination but rather on the relationships between intensities at its edges.

In the vision literature, the illusion illustrated in figure 11.9 is often misrepresented as in figure 11.10, as though a region has only one edge.

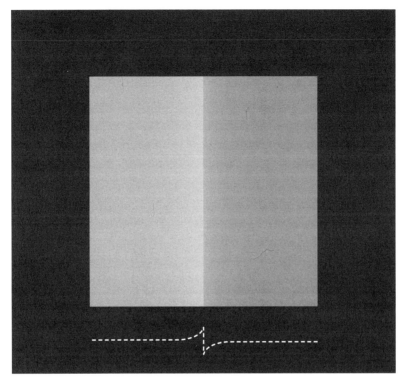

Figure II.10. A frequently studied and discussed but mistaken version of the illusion in figure II.9.

The plot below simply omits the other edges. Of course every region is surrounded on all sides by edges, so the interpretation of the appearance of patterns like the one in figure II.10 becomes confusing, because it depends on the characteristics of the actual edges in the display, which are often things like the edges of the page on which the illusion is presented.

It turns out that mechanisms consistent with what we know of the workings of the nervous system and that are not very complex can do exactly what is needed to explain the illusion in figure II.9 (and hundreds of similar ones). Here is a description of such a set of

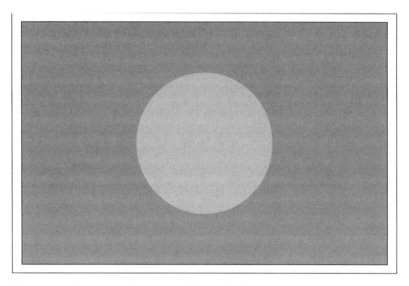

Figure 11.11. A repeat of figure 11.3 without the dots.

mechanisms. This particular set may not correctly represent how the human visual system actually operates, but it is an illustration of the fact that processes that seem extremely complex may consist of combinations of fairly simple actions that the nervous system is known to be able to perform.

Suppose you are looking at the pattern in figure 11.11. The graph at the upper left in figure 11.12 is a plot of the intensity of the retinal image across the middle of figure 11.11 when it is illuminated with light of an arbitrary intensity, and the graph at the upper right is a plot when that illumination intensity is doubled. All the light levels simply double.

A row of receptors is drawn in the middle row of figure 11.12 Those receptors merely represent the continuous tightly packed layer of receptors lying under the retinal image of the pattern in figure 11.11, each of which converts the strength of its input into an output signal proportional to the logarithm of its input. In the figure, only five receptors are drawn, and there is spacing between their representations. The

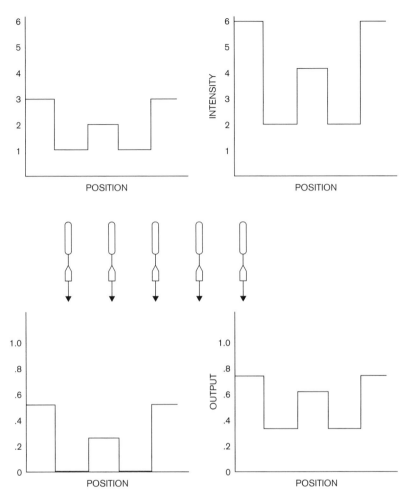

Figure 11.12. The effect of a logarithmic-like early stage in retinal processing.

way those five receptors are drawn does not represent the actual spacing or size of receptors in relation to the plots of the stimulus patterns in the top and bottom rows. In the retina, the receptors are packed tightly right next to each other, and, if you are viewing the pattern in figure 11.11 from a distance of about two feet, the retinal image of the central, light-gray disk covers a region with a diameter including about 600 cones (for a total of almost 300,000 cones under the whole image of the central disk).

In the bottom row of figure 11.12 are plots of the outputs of the logarithmic stage. Note that when the illumination on figure 11.11 is doubled (the upper-left and upper-right plots in figure 11.12), the difference in signal levels between the center and the annulus doubles, but after the logarithmic step (the lower-left and lower-right plots), doubling the illumination does not change the difference. As discussed at length in chapter 6, this provides an explanation of one form of "illusion," brightness constancy.

In figure 11.13, the top plot represents the output of the stage in figure 11.12. Next, a stage, in the middle, produces what is called *center-surround antagonism*. Each unit sends an excitatory signal "downward" toward its optic nerve fiber, and it also sends inhibitory signals to all of its neighbors. (Inhibition is represented by the small solid circles.) Although it is not represented in figure 11.13, the inhibitory signal weakens with distance, so widely separated units do not affect each other. Further, the sum of all the inhibitory signals arriving at each unit equals the amount of the excitatory signal, so that when the illumination is the same on a group of neighboring units, the net signal out of each unit, or channel, equals zero.

The result of this relatively simple arrangement is plotted in the bottom row of figure 11.13. At first glance, the result may seem strange, but it makes sense. In any large region over which the intensity is the same, the total inhibition arriving at each channel equals the excitation, so the output is zero. As an edge is approached where the intensity increases, the amount of inhibition coming from the more intense region increases, so the output is driven negative. As an edge is approached where the intensity decreases, the amount of inhibition decreases, so the output increases. But at all points far from edges, the excitation and inhibition cancel each other, producing a pattern that consists of regions of zero excitation, corresponding to uniformly intense areas, with cusps at edges. (The intensity-dependent spread model of visual processing, mentioned in chapter 10, can be substituted for both the logarithmic and

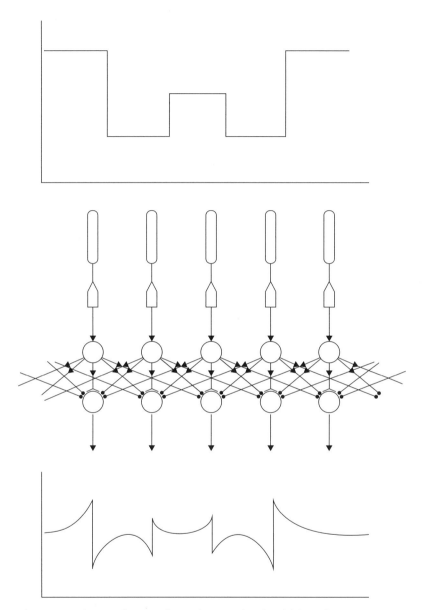

Figure 11.13. A second stage of neural processing in which each receptor excites a corresponding cell and inhibits each of its surrounding cells.

the inhibitory stages of the model in figure 11.13. It produces the same effects as those two stages.)

The strengths of all signals within uniformly illuminated regions are equal (and zero in this illustration). Actual neural signals cannot, of course, be negative. The negative portions of the plots represent inhibition and can be subtracted from the quantum mechanical background neural activity. Only near edges does the signal strength vary. (If you are familiar with digital image processing, you will recognize this as closely related to the convolution of the image with a Mexican hat function, a common step in computer image processing. If you are familiar with darkroom photographic manipulations, you will recognize what is called unsharp masking. It is also closely related to a step in what, in engineering, is called bandwidth compression.) There is ample electrophysiological evidence that a stage that produces this kind of action exists in the eyes of almost every member of the animal kingdom that has eyes, although the particular neural arrangement represented in figure 11.13 is just one of several that can have the same effect. One way to describe the effect is to say that when a photoreceptor is illuminated, the strength of the signal from the neuronal unit it drives increases, but when a neighboring receptor is illuminated instead, the strength of the output of the first unit decreases. A receptor that behaves like that is said to exhibit center-surround antagonism.

The intensity pattern plotted in the bottom row of figure 11.13 is similar to the one on the left in figure 11.9. Of course, a step in light intensity occurs when a region having one uniform intensity borders another having a different uniform intensity. When such a step is the input to a stage like the middle one in figure 11.13, the output pattern is like the bottom one in that figure. Steps turn into cusps, and all uniform regions produce the same, here zero, level of activity. It is also true that when a pattern of cusps, like the bottom plot in figure 11.13, is input to a stage like the middle one in figure 11.13, the output pattern looks very similar to the input. Each input cusp produces a similar output cusp. An input pattern like the bottom plot in figure 11.13 produces an output pattern that looks just like it (although of somewhat smaller amplitude). So if there is a stage in the human visual system that acts like the one in figure 11.13—and much evidence indicates that there is—that stage provides an explanation for one of the two aspects of the illusion in figure 11.9, that the two patterns in figure 11.9 look almost the same, even though the actual patterns are different.

Now consider the other aspect of the illusion in figure 11.9, that both patterns look like what would be expected for the light distribution on the right rather than the one on the left. Clearly, the plot at the bottom of figure 11.13 does not look like a plot of the cross-section of the brightness of the pattern in figure 11.9. ("Brightness" is the perceptual effect, as contrasted with "intensity," which is a physical measure of light level.) If the brightness of the central disk in figure 11.9 is to look different from its background, the neural activity corresponding to the center should be different from the activity corresponding to the background, so something is missing from the model. What is missing is a stage that produces what is called, inelegantly, filling-in.

It turns out that this filling-in can be accomplished by adding a relatively simple stage, as shown in figure 11.14. The plot in the top row is a redrawing of the output from the stages in figure 11.13, as the input to the stage in figure 11.14. In figure 11.14, each channel adds a portion of its signal to the outputs of its neighboring channels. Not indicated in figure 11.14 is that the strength of each of those lateral signals equals its input signal divided by the number of neighbors to which the signal is flowing, so that the total signal fed back to each channel equals the average of its neighbors. It is kind of the opposite of the stage in figure 11.13. In figure 11.13 each channel sends inhibition forward to its neighbors, while in the filling-in stage, each channel sends excitation backward to its neighbors, and the result is the opposite of the cusping that results from the inhibitory stage.

This theory or model of neural processing produces correct answers but does not necessarily represent what is actually happening in the human eye. There may be many ways of connecting the activities of

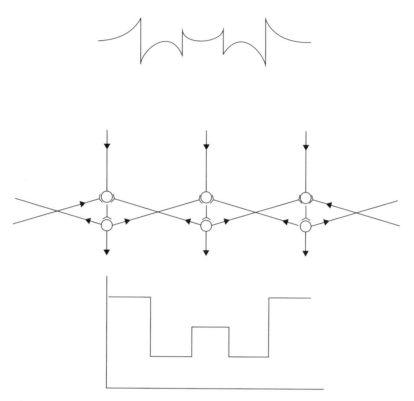

Figure 11.14. A final stage in this model of neural processing, in which each cell excites a corresponding cell and also adds excitation to the neighboring cells. This stage performs filling-in.

neural elements to produce the same result. However, the layered appearance of the histological section of retina in figure 11.6 is certainly consistent with the general idea that such processing could occur in successive stages, and electrophysiological studies of the mammalian visual system also indicate that the kinds of actions in this model do occur. (It would make evolutionary sense, in terms of reducing the activity that must travel up the optic nerves, if the final, filling-in stage occurs in the brain rather than the retina.) In any case, a model using plausible neural elements does exist that explains the phenomena that are too often "explained" by saying, in effect, that the brain figures it out.

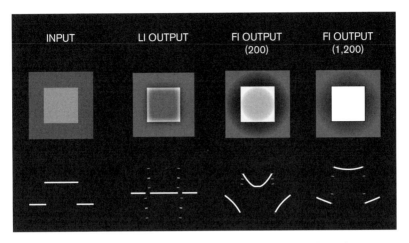

Figure 11.15. The results of the model after 100, 200, and 1,200 iterations.

Figure 11.15 shows the results of the model in figures 11.12, 11.13, and 11.14 when the target is a simple light-gray square on a darker-gray background. Note that while the general signal flow in the model is from receptors toward the optic nerve, some of the signals in the filling-in stage (figure 11.14) go backward. That means that the process in this stage is iterative, that is, it is continuously repeated; as the signal passes through this filling-in stage, it is changed; that changed signal then passes through the stage and is changed again; and the process repeats. Figure 11.15 shows some of the changes as the model iterates over time. The image labeled LI OUTPUT shows the output of the stage in the model drawn in figure 11.13, the stage that extracts edges. FI OUTPUT (200) shows the output of the final stage of the model after 200 iterations, and FI OUTPUT (1200) is the output pattern after 1,200 iterations. (The number of iterations required to produce a given output pattern depends on the parameters that happen to be chosen. For example, if the inhibition in the edge-extracting stage is assumed to spread more widely than the "nearest neighbor" spreads used in the calculations for figure 11.15, fewer iterations will be required to reach the 1,200-iteration FI OUTPUT pattern in figure 11.15.)

Because it performs filling-in, and because a cusped input to the edge-extracting stage causes a cusped output from that stage, this model also represents a possible explanation for the appearance of patterns like the ones in figure 11.9. That is, it provides an explanation for the fact that the central disks in both patterns have uniform brightnesses rather than appearing cusped.

The model generates output patterns that are consistent with the appearance of almost all of the brightness illusions that have been described in the literature. There is a class of patterns, though, all containing repetitive patterns like stripes or checkerboards, for which the model does not give correct predictions. In the model as described so far, it has been assumed that the inhibition in the edge-extracting stage spreads only to each receptor's two nearest neighbors in each direction (as drawn in figure 11.13). However, if the model is modified so that different channels spread their inhibition over different distances—and there is ample evidence that they do in real mammalian retinas—then the model makes predictions that match the appearance of these repetitive patterns as well.

Figure 11.16 is an example. The gray stripes in the left half of the pattern at the bottom of this figure are surrounded by white stripes, while the gray stripes on the right side (the identical shade of gray) are surrounded by dark stripes. By classical contrast it should be expected that the gray stripes on the left side, being surrounded by light stripes, should appear darker than the identical gray stripes on the right side, but their actual appearance is the opposite. (This has been called *assimilation,* as contrasted with *contrast*.) The plot shows that the model, as modified so that different channels spread their inhibition over different distances, predicts that the brightness of the gray stripes on the left, represented by the larger dots, will be darker initially, as would be expected from standard contrast, but after about 200 iterations the gray stripes on the left side become brighter.

The combination of all the stages in the model produces a neural output pattern that, after some iterations, agrees with the visual appearance

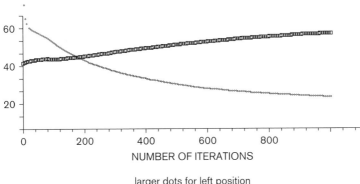

larger dots for left position

Figure 11.16. The results of the model of the scene displayed below the plot, in which a uniform gray background is covered on the left by a set of lighter stripes and on the right by a set of darker stripes. The vertical axis of the plot represents the strength of excitation, the larger dots representing the excitation of the gray regions on the left and the smaller dots the excitation of the gray regions on the right.

of the input pattern, produces output patterns that depend only on what is happening at edges, performs filling-in, and accounts for both contrast and assimilation.

However, the model does not include a mechanism to explain the *disappearance* of stabilized images. Of course light and dark adaptation will reduce the differences in outputs between, for example, regions under the shadow of a blood vessel and the unshadowed neighboring regions, but blood vessels, and all stabilized images, disappear completely within a fraction of a second, too quickly and too completely to be explained by adaptation. To account for disappearance, there must be some additional stage that passes only temporal changes in its input. If a stage is added in which each channel both excites and inhibits a following stage and the inhibitory signal is delayed relative to the excitatory path, then the excitatory signal will pass through during the delay, before the inhibition arrives and cancels it out.

Figures 11.12, 11.13, and 11.14 describe a model, a theory, which may or may not be correct, but which demonstrates that some relatively simple and plausible neural mechanisms can explain what appear to be complex visual phenomena, mechanisms that convert an array of rates of absorption of photons into visual experiences that correspond to the physical properties of objects in the world.

THINGS TO THINK ABOUT

The human peripheral retina, that is, the region of the retina away from the fovea, is extremely sensitive to any quick movement of small parts of the scene, things like birds or rabbits or floaters. Yet, in the normal human, abrupt (saccadic) eye movements occur several times every second, and each eye movement moves the retinal image of the entire scene quickly across the retina. Can you figure out a neural mechanism or set of mechanisms that might respond to small patches of movement but not to movement of the entire retinal image?

RELEVANT READING

A technical discussion of a large number of topics in vision:

Helga Kolb, Ralph Nelson, Eduardo Fernandez, and Bryan Jones (eds.). 2011. *Webvision: The Organization of the Retina and Visual System*. http://webvision. med.utah.edu.

An excellent and thorough discussion of the anatomical and physiological aspects of vision:

R. W. Rodieck. 1998. *The First Steps in Seeing*. Sunderland, MA: Sinauer Associates.

EPILOGUE

Most people would agree that the best test of true understanding is the ability to make correct predictions. Science has changed many peoples' views of the world—the earth is not the center of the universe—even bugs too small to see with the unaided eye can cause disease—vision is enabled by light rays coming into the eye rather than by rays emerging from the eye—the earth was created 4.5 billion years ago, not a few thousand. The evolution of the human brain has led us to use science and engineering to overcome many of the limitations of our physiology. But the battle continues between people who accept the assertions of proclaimed authorities and those who rely on the conclusions that emerge when logic and evidence are woven together.

REFRACTION BY WAVES

In the text, the ways that refraction affects light are illustrated in terms of rays. Although ray diagrams can be drawn to show the *effects* of refraction, they don't provide a way of understanding *why* refraction happens. Rays are defined as the paths of photons, "particles" of energy, but refraction requires some kind of interaction among neighboring regions of a light beam, and separate particles, by definition, do not interact. However, when light is thought of as waves, that is, when the wave-like properties of a beam of light are considered, the reasons why refraction must necessarily occur become evident.

Imagine a point emitting light, and imagine the light as waves, like the water waves that radiate from a pea dropped in a bathtub. Assume that the medium through which the wave travels is homogeneous. Then each point on the wave will travel away from the source at the same speed, and the wave will be an expanding sphere (or a circle when drawn as the cross-section of a spherical wave).

First, the question of why waves travel along straight paths in a homogeneous medium will be addressed. The answer seems obvious, but the process actually turns out to be a difficult one to understand. Once it is understood, refraction, the bending of waves when they pass through interfaces between different media, follows naturally.

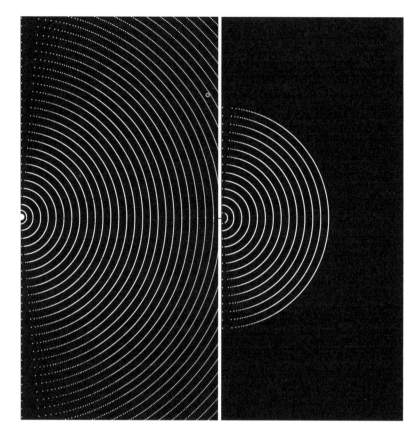

Figure A-1. Light emitted from a small source and then passing through a small hole.

Consider one point on the crest of a water wave. The water molecules at the top of the crest are pulled downward by gravity and therefore push molecules below them away, but it seems that only the molecules in the direction of travel of the wave are affected. Why doesn't each point on the crest radiate a new wave that goes off in all directions instead of just straight ahead?

Figure A-1 illustrates what happens when all points on a wave except one are blocked. The unblocked point generates a new wave. And that

Figure A-2. Light emitted from a small source and then passing through two small holes.

will happen for any single unblocked point on the wave. It is as though each point on a wave, as it travels along, generates a new set of waves. But then why does there seem to be just one single wave, instead of multiple waves spreading in all directions?

Figure A-2 illustrates what happens when there are two holes that are open. This figure illustrates the result of a phenomenon that occurs as a result of the property of waves, called *interference*. The line is a plot of the intensity of the light as it might fall on a screen, and the variation in intensity is as shown at the far right.

Interference may be best explained by reference to figure A-3. Two waves, of equal frequency and amplitude, and almost in phase, that is, going up and down almost at the same time, are plotted at the top. Note that the amplitude of each, plotted on the vertical axis, is about 100 units. In the lower plot, the two waves are just added together, and the amplitude of their sum is about 200 units. (The vertical scale in the lower plot is half that of the upper plot.) In physics, this is called by the oxymoron *constructive interference*.

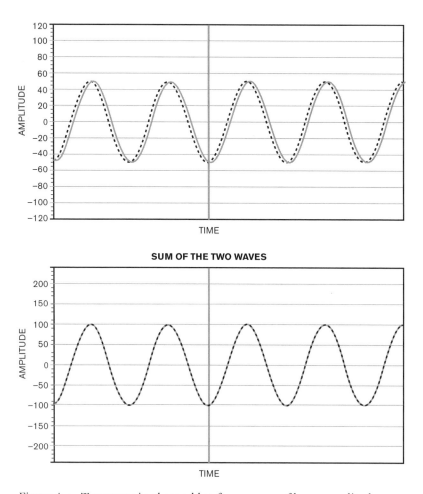

Figure A-3. Two waves in phase add to form a wave of larger amplitude.

In figure A-4, the same two waves are plotted, except that the phase of one has been shifted with respect to the other. The result is that the amplitude of their sum is reduced to about 100.

In figure A-5, the phase difference is almost 180 degrees, and the sum is almost zero. (If the phase difference were exactly 180 degrees, the sum would equal zero, and so would not illustrate the point quite as easily.) This is an example of *destructive interference*. Notice that the

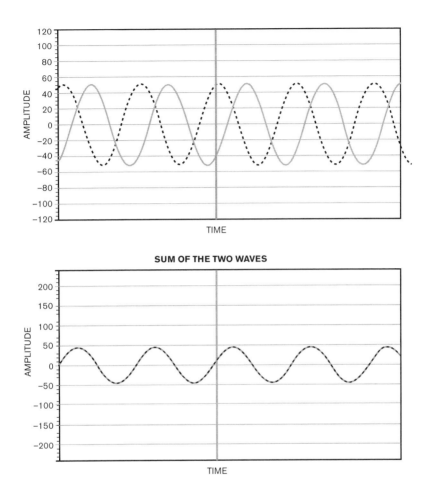

SUM OF THE TWO WAVES

Figure A-4. Two waves somewhat out of phase also add to form a new wave.

phase relation between the two waves would change if the two were initially in phase but one traveled farther than the other before they interfered.

Now look again at figure A-1. There is a small hole in the "wall" that the wave encounters, and that small portion of the wave generates a new wave. This, and most of the other figures in this appendix, were created by a computer program, and the waves do what they do not just because

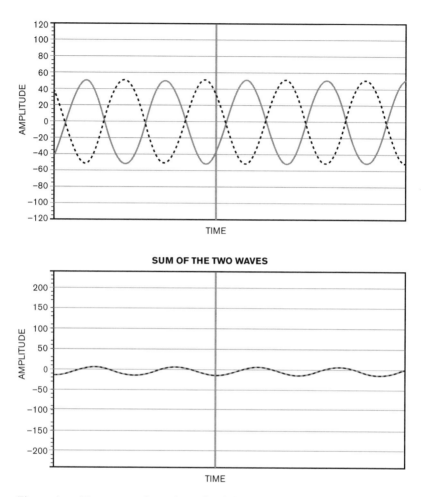

SUM OF THE TWO WAVES

Figure A-5. Two waves of equal amplitude but 180 degrees out of phase cancel each other.

the program was written to do that. The program was actually written in such a way that *every* point on *every* wave generates a new wave that starts to radiate out in all directions, but, for the reasons explained below, the waves from neighboring points interfere with each other in such a way that the wave as a whole seems to travel only straight ahead, that is, in a direction perpendicular to the tangent to the wave at its location.

Figure A-6. (A copy of figure A-2.) Light from a small source passing through two holes interferes constructively in some places and destructively in others, depending on the phase relationship between the light passing through the two holes, that is, the difference in distance each wave travels.

Here is figure A-2 again, repeated as A-6 for convenience. The waves passing through the two holes in the "wall" have traveled the same distance when they hit the place indicated by the horizontal line, and so their amplitudes are added. But a little above and below that location, the two waves have traveled through different distances, and at some height above and below the horizontal line, one wave has traveled exactly half a wavelength farther than the other, so the two waves cancel, and the amplitude is zero. In the figure, there are three different heights at which the two waves have traveled though distances such that they arrive in phase, and at other distances the two waves are almost 180 degrees out of phase. And because the waves from each hole are expanding and therefore delivering less energy per inch, the intensity falls toward zero everywhere as the distance from the horizontal line increases.

Figure A-1 showed light passing through a tiny hole. Light arriving at a screen on the far side of the hole would spread widely, its intensity falling off in proportion to the distance from the hole. Figure A-7 shows

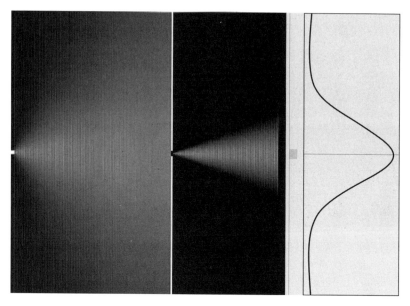

Figure A-7. Light from a small source passing through a hole somewhat larger than in figure A-1.

the distribution of light passing through a hole that is a little bigger than the hole in figure A-1. The light spreads less widely.

Figure A-8 shows what happens if the hole is even larger. (Please ignore the little ripples in the plot and the streaks in the plot on the right of the hole. They are artifacts of the fact that, although a real wave must be considered as an infinite number of neighboring points, each of which generates a new wave, the program that generates these plots must compute the result from a sampling, that is, a finite number, of these points. These ripples, then, are evidence that the program was actually written to generate a wave at each of a representative set of points on the wave, simulating how light actually behaves, rather than simply drawing a picture of what is known to occur.) As the hole gets larger, a *beam* of light is developed.

Here's what's happening. Remember that each point on a wave acts as though it were generating a new wave that spreads in all directions.

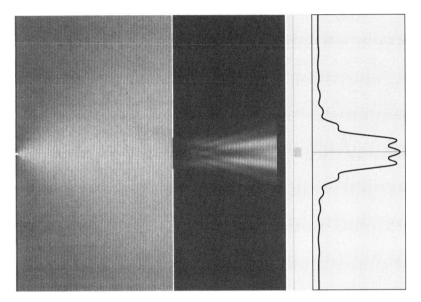

Figure A-8. Light from a small source passing through an even larger hole, forming a beam. The ripples are artifacts of the method used to compute the figure. If an infinite number of points were used in the computation, the curve would be smooth.

Consider any two points in the hole such that the upper point and the lower one are at equal distances from the center of the hole. At any distance to the right of the hole, the waves passing through those two points will have traveled through equal distances, so they will constructively interfere and produce an intensity that is the maximum that the sum of the two waves can have. The same is true for all pairs of points in the hole that are equal distances from the center, and those maximal intensities will all add to each other. However, waves through any pair of points not equally distant from the center will produce a sum that is less than maximal, and some will produce a sum of zero.

Waves that pass through near the center of the hole will generate new waves that pass straight ahead, and the parts of those waves that would be expected to spread out sideways meet destructive interference from the waves generated by neighboring points, while waves generated by points near the edges of the hole spread out more, because there are fewer neighboring waves to interfere with them. The result is a beam that travels straight ahead, has a more or less flat leading edge, and spreads at its edges.

The meaning of the term *leading edge* (of the beam) is probably obvious in that context, but the term used to refer to it in optics is *wavefront*. The wavefront formed by a single point source has a circular (or spherical) shape, and the farther the wave has traveled, the closer the wavefront is to a straight line (or flat surface), traveling in a direction perpendicular to itself. When the paths of photons from a distant point source are represented by rays, the rays from the point source are parallel. (Of course, rays from point sources in different directions, or from different points on a surface that reflects light, will be parallel to other rays from the same point but will not be parallel to rays from other points.)

That (hopefully) explains why, even though each point on a wavefront can be thought of as generating a new wave that travels in all directions, light seems to travel in beams. But the beams are only straight when the light is traveling through a homogeneous medium, that is, a medium in which it travels at the same speed everywhere. When, instead, a beam encounters a surface between two media in which light travels at differing speeds, the direction of the beam may change. If the beam strikes the surface while traveling in a direction perpendicular to the surface, or, to put it another way, if the wavefront is parallel to the surface, the waves will change their speed, but the relationships among their phases will not change. Pairs of points equidistant from the center of the beam will still be in phase, and points near the edges of the beam will have fewer waves destructively interfering with them, so the beam will continue to travel in the same direction, spreading only at its edges. The rays will be straight—the amount of change in the direction of the beam will be zero.

However, if the beam is incident on the surface at an angle that is not perpendicular to the surface, then the direction of travel will change: *refraction.* That is illustrated in figure A-9, where light passing through air (practically the same speed as in vacuum) intersects a flat glass surface at an angle. The beam of light is traveling from left to right. The lines perpendicular to the direction of travel represent various positions of the wavefront as it travels, and the diagonal sets of lines that join at a point indicate pairs of waves, *a* with *a, b* with *b,* and so on, that travel through equal distances and therefore form the beam.

At the instant when the point × enters the glass, the light at point *y,* at the other end of its wavefront, has already traveled through a small distance in the glass. Therefore, as soon as the beam begins to enter the glass, the angle for which the pairs of waves are in phase changes, so the wavefront changes its angle. Obviously, the greater the amount by which the light slows down, the greater is the change in angle. Also, the greater the angle between the incident wavefront and the surface, the greater will be the change in angle. As a consequence of the change in the speed of the light (and the fact that photons have no memory), the waves, in the glass, will have a higher frequency and shorter wavelength than when they were in air, but they will carry no information about the angle at which they traveled before they entered the glass. (If you consider light as a stream of photons, each photon carries more energy, but fewer photons pass each point per second.)

In figure A-9, the light passes into a medium in which it is slowed down. The same geometry applies when light enters a medium in which it speeds up, for example when the light passes from glass to air, and, of course, the beam bends the opposite way.

You might want to think of a photon as a tiny spherical disturbance occupying a region about the size of its wavelength and carrying only the information of its frequency. Wherever it is, it doesn't keep track of where it's been or what direction it's traveling. It just generates a wave that spreads out in all directions at a speed that depends on the medium it is in, and whatever happens to the parts of the wave, such as being interfered with by other waves, just happens.

But, you say, waves traveling in space pass right through each other, they don't interact with each other until they hit a place where they are

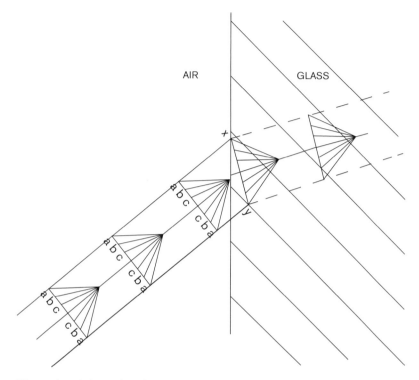

AIR

GLASS

Figure A-9. The paths of rays are determined by the interference among neighboring rays.

absorbed and detected, so how could the waves that travel out sideways in a beam cancel neighbors that are not in phase? Right, but how do you know, for instance, that there *is* a beam unless it is detected? Aarrrg. We just stepped into another one of those deep places.

An equation for the actual relationships among the angle of incidence of the waves, the amount by which their speed is changed, and the amount by which their direction of travel changes, can be straightfor-wardly derived from the geometric and trigonometric relationships that are described above. The relationship is called Snell's law. As shown in figure A-10, define AI as the angle of incidence—the angle between the direction of travel of the waves heading for the surface and the perpen-

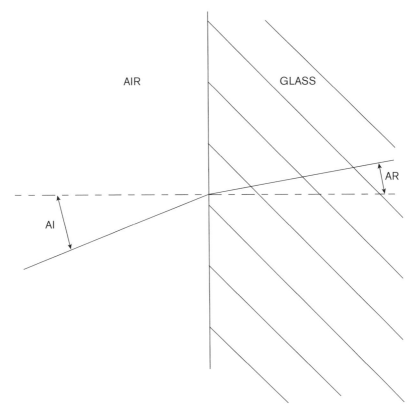

Figure A-10. The definitions of the quantities in Snell's Law.

dicular to the surface. Define AR as the angle of refraction—the angle between the direction of travel after the wave front has entered the second medium and the perpendicular to the surface. Then:

sin(AI)/sin(AR) = (speed of wave in the second medium)/(speed of wave in the first medium).

SELECTED BIBLIOGRAPHY

Baylor, D.A. 1987. "Photoreceptor Signals and Vision. Proctor Lecture." *Investigative Ophthalmology and Visual Science* 28: 34–49. (Excellent discussion of the effects of light on photoreceptor pigment.)

Cornsweet, T.N. 1962. "Changes in the Appearance of Stimuli of Very High Luminance." *Psychological Review* 69: 257–73.

Cornsweet, T. N., H. Fowler, R.G. Rabedeau, R.E. Whalen, and D.R. Williams. 1958. "Changes in the Perceived Color of Very Bright Stimuli." *Science* 128: 898–99.

Cornsweet, T.N., and J.I. Yellott. 1985. "Intensity-Dependent Spatial Summation." *Journal of the Optical Society of America A* 2: 1769–86.

Feynman, Richard Phillips, Robert B. Leighton, and Matthew Sands. 1963. *The Feynman Lectures on Physics.* Addison-Wesley. (Even though it is more than fifty years old, for a clear explanation of the physical principles underlying optics (and for all of physics), there is nothing better than the Feynman Lectures.)

Kolb, Helga, Ralph Nelson, Eduardo Fernandez, and Bryan Jones (eds.). 2011. *Webvision: The Organization of the Retina and Visual System.* http://webvision.med.utah.edu. (A technical discussion of a large number of topics in vision.)

Liversedge, Simon P., Iain D. Gilchrist, and Stefan Everling (eds.). 2011. *Oxford Handbook of Eye Movements.* Oxford: Oxford University Press. (Comprehensive coverage of research on eye movements.)

Rodieck, R. W. 1998. *The First Steps in Seeing.* Sunderland, MA: Sinauer Associates. (An excellent and thorough discussion of the anatomical and physiological aspects of vision.)

Saari, J. C. 2000. "Biochemistry of Visual Pigment Regeneration: The Friedenwald Lecture." *Investigative Ophthalmology and Visual Science* 41: 337–48. (The
biochemistry of visual pigment regeneration [from straight to bent].)

Treutwein, Bernhard. 1995. "Adaptive Psychophysical Procedures." *Vision
Research* 35: 2503–22. (A review of modern methods for psychophysical data
collection.)

INDEX

Note: Figures are indicated by *f* after the page number.

absorption of photons, 20–24, 34; and excitation of optic nerve fiber, 59–60
absorption spectrum(a), 21–23, 22*f*, 23*f*; of cones, 114–17, 115*f*; of rods, 111–12, 112*f*
accommodation, 100–106, 102*f*, 103*f*
adaptation: dark, 11, 17, 26, 39–40, 70–71; light, 11, 17, 26
adaptive optics, 44
afterimages, 40–41, 42, 149
amplitude, 5, 8
angle of incidence, 176–78, 178*f*
aqueous humor, 14, 91
arteries, 44, 45*f*
arterioles, 44, 45*f*
assimilation, 162
astigmatism, 104–5
atoms, 7
auras, migraine, 109
autorefractor, 96
axis, 105

background, intensity of, 150, 150*f*
bandwidth compression, 158

B cones: absorption spectrum of, 114–17, 115*f*; missing, 118
beam of light, 174–79; change of direction of, 176–79, 178*f*, 179*f*; development of, 174–75, 175*f*; and interference, 175–76; leading edge of, 176; wave-like properties of, 167
bifocals, 101, 106
bleached pigment molecules, 11, 21, 25–26, 37–39, 60
bleaching rate: and excitation of optic nerve fiber, 60, 67; for five different intensities, 62, 63*f*; for four different rates of unbleaching, 65, 65*f*; for higher intensities, 62–63, 64*f*; after leveling off for five rates of unbleaching, 67–69, 68*f*; oscillation of, 68–69; and range of intensities, 60–61
blood vessels of eye, 43–49, 44*f*–46*f*, 48*f*; shadows of, 46–49, 48*f*, 144–48, 144*f*, 145*f*, 147*f*
blur circles: and accommodation, 101–4; in hypermetropia, 97–99, 98*f*; in photograph, 86–89, 88*f*, 90

bonds, 15
brain afterimages, 41
brightness: in color vision, 127–28, 132; and intensity of background, 150, 150*f*; limitation in, 3; relative, 71; role of pupil in, 16–18
brightness constancy, 50–58; and color constancy, 58; example of, 50–52, 51*f*; as illusion, 149–50, 156; and intensity-dependent summation, 56–57; logarithmic relationship in, 52–58, 53*f*–55*f*; and Weber's law, 57–58

camera, light sensing by, 26–27
capillaries, 44, 45*f*, 47, 49
cataracts, 107–8
center-surround antagonism, 156–59, 157*f*
choroid, 147, 147*f*
color blindness: colors seen in, 126–31, 128*f*; defined, 127; total, 113–14, 118
color constancy, 58, 133–35
color differences, interocular, 109–10
color names, 126
color triangles, 127
color vision, 111–36; absorption spectra of cones in, 114–17, 115*f*; absorption spectrum of rods in, 111–12, 112*f*; adjustment of intensity in, 120–21, 121*f*; brightness, hue, and saturation in, 127–29, 129*f*, 131–33, 131*f*; color constancy in, 58, 133–35; color names in, 126; colors seen by color-blind people in, 126–31, 128*f*; with cones with three different absorption spectra, 122, 122*f*, 131–33, 131*f*; in dim light, 114; evolution of three rather than just two pigments in, 123; naming of visual pigment in, 116–17; with only rods, 111, 113–14, 113*f*, 118; with only rods and G cones, 118; with only two types of cones, 118–21, 119*f*, 121*f*, 129–31, 130*f*, 131*f*; reason for not evolving more than

three kinds of cones in, 123–26; requiring two photons to be absorbed in same receptor in, 117; and wavelength blindness, 113–14, 118; and wavelength of photon, 112–13
color wheels, 127
cones, 3; absorption spectra of, 114–17, 115*f*; color vision with all three types of, 122, 122*f*, 131–33, 131*f*; color vision with only two types of, 118–21, 119*f*, 121*f*, 129–31, 130*f*, 131*f*; at low illumination levels, 70; people whose retinas contain no, 70; in plane of focus, 103–4; unbleaching rate of, 69–70
constructive interference, 169, 169*f*, 170*f*, 173, 173*f*
contact lenses, 14, 15*f*, 18
contrast effect, 150–51, 151*f*
cornea, 14, 15*f*, 18, 91
corpuscles, 47
crystalline lens. *See* lens
curvature requirement, 105
cusps, 158–59
cylindrical lens, 104–5
cylindrical power, 105

dark adaptation: defined, 11, 17, 26; and seeing things that aren't there, 39–40; sensitivity of human retina in, 27–34, 29*f*–32*f*; unbleaching of pigment molecules and, 70–71
darkness, streak of light in, 42
dark room, flashes seen in, 37–39
destructive interference, 170–71, 171*f*–173*f*, 173
deuteranopia, 122
diabetic retinopathy, 144, 144*f*
dim light: color vision in, 114; flicker in, 68–69
disappearance of stabilized image, 141–49; and afterimages, 149; and blood-vessel shadows, 141–48, 144*f*, 145*f*, 147*f*; evolutionary advantage of,

148–49; examples of, 141–43, 142*f*; and model of neural processing, 163–64; and small eye movements, 143–44

edge extraction, 148, 161, 162
electromagnetic waves, 2, 6–12
electrons, 7
electron shifts, 9
energy: defined, 5, 7; kinetic, 7; potential, 7; and wavelengths in photon, 21
energy levels, 9
eye: anatomy of, 14–18, 15*f*; vascular structure of, 43–49, 44*f*–46*f*, 48*f*
eye examination. *See* vision examination
eyeglasses, examination for. *See* vision examination
eye movements, 92–94; tiny, 137–41, 138*f*, 140*f*
eyes closed: afterimages with, 40–41; sparkles seen with, 36–40

farsightedness, 97, 98*f*
filling-in, 159, 160*f*
flashes: seen in dark room, 37–39; seen with eyes closed, 36–40
flicker in dim light, 68–69
floaters, 108–9
fluorescence, 45, 46*f*, 49
focus, plane of, 100–101, 103–4
force, 5, 6–7
fovea, 14, 15*f*; and retinal blood vessels, 44, 45*f*; in retinal image formation, 93–94, 103–4
frequency, 5, 8

ganglion cells, 147, 147*f*
G cones: absorption spectrum of, 114–17, 115*f*; color vision with only rods and, 118; color vision with R and, 118–21, 119*f*, 121*f*; missing, 122
glass, rays passing through, 74–75, 74*f*

glasses, examination for. *See* vision examination
glint, 91
graininess, 40

hue, 127–28, 132
hue intensity (HI) constance, 133–34
hue wavelength-composition (HW) constance, 133, 134–35
hypermetropia, 97, 98*f*

IDS (intensity-dependent summation), 56–57
illusions, 150–54; brightness constancy as, 149–50, 156; contrast effect as, 150–51, 151*f*; defined, 150; with different reflectances, 151–54, 152*f*, 153*f*; effect of intensity of background on brightness as, 150, 150*f*
image: definition of, 90; distance from lens of, 102–3, 102*f*, 103*f*; magnification of, 85–86, 86*f*; of source, 73. *See also* disappearance of stabilized image
image formation, retinal, 91–92, 91*f*, 97
incident light, 36–37
infrared light, 125–26
inner nuclear layer, 147*f*
inner plexiform layer, 147*f*
intensity(ies): of background and brightness, 150, 150*f*; bleaching rate for five different, 62, 63*f*; bleaching rate for higher, 62–63, 64*f*; and color vision, 120–21, 121*f*; differences in responses to different levels of, 66, 145–46, 145*f*; logarithm of, 69, 145–46, 145*f*; response of retina to very high, 67; response of retina to very low, 66–67
intensity-dependent summation (IDS), 56–57
intensity range, 10–11, 26; bleaching rate and, 60–61

interference, 169–72, 169f–172f;
    constructive, 169, 169f, 170f, 173, 173f;
    destructive, 170–71, 171f–173f, 173
interocular color differences, 109–10
intraocular lens (IOL), 108
iris, 14, 15f, 16
isomers, 20, 20f, 24
iterative process, 161, 161f

kinetic energy, 7

L cones, 114–17, 115f
leading edge, 176–77
lens(es): accommodation of, 100–106,
    102f, 103f; anatomy of, 14, 15f, 18;
    cataracts of, 107–8; curvature and
    thickness of, 83–85, 83f–85f;
    cylindrical, 104–5; distance of image
    from, 102–3, 102f, 103f; distribution of
    light at different distances from, 86,
    87f; and image formation, 79–81, 80f,
    81f; intraocular, 108; "negative," 100f;
    in phoropter, 97–98, 98f; progressive,
    106; in retinal image formation, 91;
    scleral, 139–41, 140f
light: background about, 4–12;
    distribution at different distances
    from lens of, 86, 87f; and other
    electromagnetic waves, 6–12; speed
    of, 73–74; as stream of particles, 73;
    water waves and, 4–5, 6f; wavelike
    properties of, 73, 89–90
light adaptation, 11, 17, 26
light intensity and receptor output,
    52–58, 53f–55f
lightness constancy, 50–58, 51f, 53f–55f
light sensing, 19–35; absorption
    spectrum in, 22–24, 23f; bleaching
    in, 21; dark and light adaptation in,
    26; isomers of visual pigments in,
    20, 20f, 24; in man-made devices,
    26–27; optic disk in, 19; quantum
    mechanics in, 25–26; sensitivity of
    dark-adapted human retina to,
    27–34, 29f–32f; and visual signal

triggered by non-visual event,
    24–25; wavelength and energy in,
    21, 22f
logarithmic relationship: in brightness
    constancy, 54–58; between light
    intensity and strength of receptor
    output, 145–46, 145f
logarithmic scale, 3, 13

macula, 14, 15f, 43
macular pigment, 48
magnification, 85–86, 86f
manual refraction, 96–106
M cones, 114–17, 115f
migraine auras, 109
myopia, 99–100, 99f, 100f

nanometers (nm), 23
nearsightedness, 99–100, 99f, 100f
negative afterimage, 40–41, 42, 149
negative charge, 8
"negative" lens, 100f
nerve fiber layer, 147, 147f
neural processing, 137–64; and
    afterimages, 149; and bandwidth
    compression, 158; of blood-vessel
    shadows, 144–48, 144f, 145f, 147f; and
    brightness constancy, 149–50;
    center-surround antagonism in,
    156–59, 157f; cusps in, 158–59; and
    disappearance of stabilized images,
    163–64; disappearance of stabilized
    images and appearance of
    unstabilized ones in, 141–49, 142f,
    163–64; edge extraction in, 148, 161,
    162; filling-in in, 159, 160f; and
    illusions, 150–54, 150f–153f; iterative,
    161, 161f; logarithmic-like early stage
    of, 154–56, 154f, 155f; models of,
    154–64, 163f; of repetitive patterns,
    162, 163f; and retinal layers, 159–60;
    tiny eye movements in, 137–41, 138f,
    140f
neurons, maximum firing rate of,
    66, 69

night-blindness, 70
non-visual event, visual signal
    triggered by, 24–25, 36–42

ocular fundus, 44f, 144f
OD, 105
ophthalmologists, 95
ophthalmoscope, 18
optic disk, 19, 43, 44f
opticians, 96
optic nerve, 15f
optic nerve fiber(s), 144, 144f;
    bleaching rate and excitation of,
    59–60, 67
optic nerve fiber layer, 147, 147f
optics, 72–94; blur circles in, 86–89, 88f;
    curvature of lens in, 83–85, 83f–85f;
    definition of image in, 90;
    distribution of light at different
    distances from lens in, 86, 87f; eye
    movements in, 92–94; lens in, 79–81,
    80f, 81f; light in, 73; magnification in,
    85–86, 86f; point source in, 72–73;
    principle of reciprocity in, 81–82;
    rays in, 74–79, 74f, 77f, 79f; refraction
    in, 75–78, 76f, 77f; retinal image
    formation in, 91–92, 91f; speed of
    light in, 73–74; wavelike properties
    of light in, 73, 89–90
optometrists, 95–96
OS, 105
outer nuclear layer, 147f
outer plexiform layer, 147f

parallel rays, 77f, 78–79, 79f
phase, waves in, 169, 170f
phase-shifted waves, 170–71, 171f
phoropter, 96; lens in, 97–98, 98f
photographs: blur circles in, 86–89, 88f,
    90; red pupils in, 82
photons: absorption of, 20–24, 22f, 23f,
    34; and anatomy of eye, 15–16;
    defined, 10; variability in emission
    of, 30–31; wavelength and energy in,
    21; wavelength of, 112–13

photoreceptor(s), 15–16, 19; sensing of
    light by, 19–35
photoreceptor layer, 147, 147f
physical world: atoms in, 7; bleaching
    of pigment molecules in, 11;
    electron shifts in, 9–10; energy in, 7;
    energy levels in, 9; force in, 6–7;
    frequency and amplitude of
    wavelengths in, 8; idea of, 1–13; light
    and dark adaptation in, 11; light and
    other electromagnetic waves in,
    6–12; photons in, 10; positive and
    negative charge in, 8; quanta in, 10;
    range of intensities in, 10–11; static
    electricity in, 7; things in, 1–2;
    visible wavelengths in, 2–3, 3f, 8–9;
    water waves in, 4–5, 6f
pigmented epithelium, 147, 147f
pigment molecules. *See* visual pigment
    molecules
plano, 105
point, 72
point source, 72–73
Poisson distribution, 30
Poisson, Simeon, 118
positive afterimage, 40, 41, 149
positive charge, 8
potential energy, 7
presbyopia, 101, 106
pressure, 19
prisms, rays passing through, 76–79,
    77f, 79f
progressive lenses, 106
protons, 7
pupil(s): anatomy of, 14, 15f; red, 82; in
    retinal image formation, 91; role in
    vision of, 16–18

quanta, 10
quantum mechanics (QM), 25–26, 30,
    37–39

rays, 74–79; bending by lens of, 79–81,
    80f, 81f; defined, 167; parallel, 77f, 78;
    passing through glass, 74–75, 74f;

passing through prisms, 76–79, 77*f,*
79*f;* path of, 177–79, 178*f,* 179*f;*
refraction of, 75–78, 76*f,* 77*f*
R cones: absorption spectrum of,
114–17, 115*f;* color vision with G and,
118–21, 119*f,* 121*f*
reading glasses, 101
receptor output, light intensity and,
52–58, 53*f*–55*f,* 145–46, 145*f*
reciprocity, principle of, 81–82
red pupils, 82
reflectances, illusions with different,
151–54, 152*f,* 153*f*
refraction: defined, 75, 96, 167; manual,
96–106; vs. rays, 167; rays and, 75–78,
76*f,* 77*f;* by waves, 167–79, 178*f,* 179*f*
repetitive patterns, 162, 163*f*
retina: anatomy of, 14, 15–16, 15*f;* image
formation on, 91–92, 91*f,* 97; layers
of, 146–48, 147*f;* responses of, 66–67;
sensitivity of dark-adapted human,
27–34, 29*f*–32*f;* vascular structure of,
43–49, 44*f*–46*f,* 48*f*
11-*cis*-retinal, 20*f*
all-*trans*-retinal, 20*f*
retinal blood vessels: anatomy of,
43–46, 44*f*–46*f;* shadows of, 46–49,
48*f,* 144–48, 144*f,* 145*f,* 147*f*
retinal tear, 109
Rodieck, Robert, 118
rods, 3; absorption spectrum in, 22–23,
23*f,* 24, 34; absorption spectrum of,
111–12, 112*f;* color vision with only,
111, 113–14, 113*f,* 118; color vision
with only G cones and, 118; people
whose retinas contain no, 70; two
states of, 25; at typical daylight
levels, 70
rotational movements, 92, 93; tiny,
137–41, 138*f,* 140*f*

saturation, 127–28, 132–33
sclera, 147, 147*f*
scleral lenses, 139–41, 140*f*

S cones, 114–17, 115*f*
sensitivity of dark-adapted human
retina, 27–34, 29*f*–32*f*
slit lamp, 106
Snell's law, 178–79, 179*f*
source, 72
sparkles: seen in dark room, 37–39; seen
with eyes closed, 36–40
spectral sensitivity curve, 26–27
stabilized image, disappearance of.
See disappearance of stabilized
image
staircase method, 33–34
static electricity, 7
steady gaze, tiny eye movements
during, 137–41, 138*f,* 140*f*
sunglasses, 71

target, disappearance of. *See*
disappearance of stabilized
image
threshold: in brightness constancy,
57–58; for seeing flash, 29–34
translations, 92–93
tritanopia, 118

ultraviolet light, 12, 125
unbleaching of pigment molecules,
25–26, 60; and dark adaptation,
70–71
unbleaching rate(s), 59–71; bleaching
rate after leveling off for five
different, 67–69, 68*f;* bleaching rate
for four different, 65, 65*f;* chemical
constituents surrounding pigment
and, 66; in cones, 69–70; factors that
may have influenced evolution of,
66–69

variability in measurement of
threshold for seeing flash, 29–31
vascular structure of eye, 43–49,
44*f*–46*f,* 48*f*
veins, 44, 45*f,* 46

visible wavelengths, 2–3, 3*f*, 8
vision examination, 95–110;
  accommodation in, 100–106, 102*f*,
  103*f*; astigmatism in, 104–5; cataracts
  in, 107–8; colors that differ between
  eyes in, 109–10; eyeglass
  prescription in, 105–6; floaters in,
  108–9; hypermetropia
  (farsightedness) in, 97, 98*f*; and
  migraine auras, 109; myopia
  (nearsightedness) in, 99–100, 99*f*,
  100*f*; presbyopia in, 101, 106; slit
  lamp, 106; tools for, 96; types of
  specialists for, 95–96
visual angle, 93
visual pigment molecules: absorption
  of photons by, 20–24, 22*f*, 23*f*;
  bleached, 11, 21, 25–26, 37–39, 60; in
  brightness constancy, 53–54;
  evolution of three, 123–26; two
  states of, 20–21, 20*f*, 25; unbleaching
  of, 25–26, 59–71
visual signal triggered by non-visual
  event, 24–25, 36–42

vitreous gel, 14, 15*f*, 108, 147
vitreous humor, 14, 15*f*, 108, 147

water waves, 4–5, 6*f*
wave(s): path of, 177–79, 178*f*, 179*f*; in
  phase, 169, 170*f*; phase-shifted,
  170–71, 171*f*; refraction by, 167–79
wavefront, 176–77
wave generation: from light passing
  through larger hole, 173–74, 174*f*,
  175*f*; from light passing through
  single hole, 168–69, 168*f*; from light
  passing through two small holes,
  169, 169*f*
wavelength(s): defined, 5, 6*f*, 8; and
  energy in photon, 21; of photon,
  112–13; visible, 2–3, 3*f*, 8
wavelength blindness, 113–14, 118
wavelike properties of light, 73,
  89–90
Weber's law, 57
white cells, 47

X-rays, 125